ALL THE NEWS IS FIT TO PRINT

ALL THE NEWS IS FIT TO PRINT

PROFILE
OF A
COUNTRY
EDITOR

CHAD STEBBINS

University of Missouri Press   *Columbia and London*

Copyright © 1998 by
The Curators of the University of Missouri
University of Missouri Press, Columbia, Missouri 65201
Printed and bound in the United States of America
All rights reserved
5 4 3 2 1   02 01 00 99 98

Library of Congress Cataloging-in-Publication Data

Stebbins, Chad, 1960–
    All the news is fit to print : profile of a country editor / Chad
Stebbins.
        p.   cm.
    Based on the author's thesis (doctoral)—Bowling Green (Ohio)
State University.
    Includes bibliographical references and index.
    ISBN 0-8262-1163-1 (alk. paper)
    1. Aull, Arthur Fabian, 1872–1948.   2. Newspaper editors—
Missouri—Biography.   3. Lamar democrat (Lamar, Mo. : 1883)
I. Title.
PN4874.A85S74   1998
070.4'1'092—dc21
[B]   97-51350
                                                                CIP

⊗ ™ This paper meets the requirements of the
American National Standard for Permanence of Paper
for Printed Library Materials, Z39.48, 1984.

Designer: Stephanie Foley
Typesetter: Crane Typesetting Service, Inc.
Printed and binder: Thomson-Shore, Inc.
Typefaces: Adobe Garamond and Aquiline

To my grandmother, Vera Boline,
who died July 22, 1996.

She would have read every word of this
book with her magnifying glass and
enjoyed it more than anyone else.

CONTENTS

ACKNOWLEDGMENTS

I am grateful to a number of people for providing assistance along the way. Foremost is Betty Aull White, who answered innumerable questions about her father and supplied a wealth of information that was not available elsewhere. Also in Lamar, I had the help of Doug Davis, current publisher of the *Democrat;* Opal Sims, who celebrated her twenty-fifth anniversary with the paper in 1996 and is the last remaining link to the Aull ownership; Dale Wootton, curator of the Barton County Historical Society; and Bob Potter, collector of historical photographs.

This book is based on my doctoral dissertation at Bowling Green (Ohio) State University. My thanks to the members of my committee: Dr. Ray Laakaniemi, Dr. Catherine Cassara, Dr. F. Dennis Hale, and Dr. Jack Thomas. I am also appreciative of Missouri Southern State College for allowing me to take a one-year leave of absence to complete the course work for my degree.

At Missouri Southern, where much of the research for this book was completed, I was assisted by circulation librarian Gaye Pate and reference librarians Mary Lou Dove, Bob Black, and Terre Hargis. I also appreciate the friendship and support of Richard Massa, head of the communications department; Dr. Allen Merriam, professor of communications; and the students in my community journalism class.

I am grateful to the State Historical Society of Missouri for the interlibrary loans of dozens of reels of microfilm; James Kirkpatrick, former Missouri secretary of state, for additional microfilm and the idea of a book on Arthur Aull; and Dr. Lawrence Christensen, one of the readers of the manuscript who recommended that the University of Missouri Press publish it. Dr. Christensen, an editor of the *Missouri Biographical Dictionary,* has included an essay on Aull in the dictionary.

At the University of Missouri Press, I enjoyed working with Beverly Jarrett, director and editor in chief; Clair Willcox, acquisitions editor; Jane Lago, managing editor; Karen Caplinger, marketing manager; and John Brenner, the editor assigned to this book. Clair, in particular, made the publication of *All the News Is Fit to Print* possible, and John caught several mistakes that I had missed despite reading the manuscript countless times.

Finally, I thank my family: wife Debbie; sons Brennan, Grant, Joel, and Samuel; parents Wayne Stebbins and Janice Stebbins; and sister Kren Harmon.

ALL THE NEWS IS FIT TO PRINT

1

THE MAKING OF AN EDITOR

> The people of this county are so accustomed to the Lamar Democrat that it is not likely they realize what an outstanding publication it is. In its field it is without equal so far as I know. It violates most of the rules and conventions of journalism and at the same time succeeds far above all those who comply. For more than forty years Arthur Aull has been the Lamar Democrat. He has written so much that his soul stands naked before us. Four or five thousand of us eagerly read his paper from beginning to end each day. His personality permeates everything in the paper.
>
> —*Fred J. Gray, state representative, December 22, 1944*

When word reached him of Arthur Aull's death on May 7, 1948, President Harry Truman declared that an "able and picturesque figure in American journalism has passed on." Truman Press Secretary Charlie Ross, a former editorial page editor and chief of the Washington bureau for the *St. Louis Post-Dispatch,* added, "As one who knew Mr. Aull from my previous Missouri newspaper connection, I would like to associate myself with this tribute."[1]

News of Aull's death was carried by newspapers ranging from the *New York Times* to the *San Francisco Examiner* and in such magazines as *Time* and *Newsweek.* The *St. Louis Post-Dispatch* reported, "So widely was he quoted in the metropolitan press and by radio and stage comedians that many thought the Lamar Daily Democrat was a mythical sheet."[2]

But the *Lamar Democrat* did exist, and for nearly half a century Arthur Aull held a rural Missouri town spellbound with his all-the-news-is-fit-to-print style of journalism. The paper boasted a circulation of four thousand—substantially larger than the population of Lamar—with readers in all forty-eight states plus Canada and England. Subscribers included W. C. Fields and O. O. McIntyre, a syndicated newspaper columnist from New York who was the most widely read writer of his era.[3]

Aull's fame began to spread nationally in the late 1920s when McIntyre and Ted Cook, a Los Angeles–based syndicated columnist, started sprinkling curious items from the *Democrat* in their columns. Soon after, unusual stories from the paper began showing up in the *New York Times,* the *New York World Telegram, The New Yorker,* and even the *Journal of the American Medical Association.*[4] Feature stories about Aull appeared in *Publishers' Auxiliary,* the *Chicago Daily News, Life, Time, American Magazine,* and *Harper's,* the latter two after his death.

Despite the national acclaim, Arthur Aull was an unpretentious country editor who abided by his own set of rules the forty-eight years he published the *Democrat.* He was sued for libel three times, assaulted with a club, threatened with other kinds of bodily harm, and cursed by many. But he persisted in printing every scandal and piece of gossip that he could turn up. He detested the syndicated material that other country papers used and insisted on filling his paper, an afternoon daily, with the stories he gathered every morning. He realized early on that newspapering was a business above all else, and that sensationalism sold papers. Consequently, his entire career was spent looking for the shocking, the scurrilous, the comical, even the grim and grisly story that might encourage someone to pick up the *Democrat.*

AULL'S EARLY YEARS

Arthur Fabian Aull was born on November 18, 1872, in Daviess County, Kentucky, near Knottsville, just a few miles south of where the Ohio River separates Kentucky from Indiana. His great-grandfather, Benjamin Aull, Sr., moved to Kentucky from Maryland around 1810 and settled in central Kentucky. In 1830 he moved with a large colony of neighbors to Daviess County, in the western part of the state. Aull's father, William, the oldest of twelve children born to Benjamin Aull, Jr. and Joan Carico, grew up on his father's farm near Knottsville. In 1871, at the age of twenty-three, William Aull married Mary Pool of Knottsville.[5]

After acquiring a majority interest in his father's farm around the time of his marriage, William Aull with his brother, Tom, bought a large general store in Knottsville. The store's failure left William Aull financially ruined and at odds with his own family. He moved his wife and young son to Sangamon County, Illinois, near Springfield, where Mary Pool Aull's family lived. William Aull worked by the month as a farm laborer but remained "practically penniless."[6] On May 31, 1876, his wife died in childbirth, leaving him with a three-year-old son to bring up alone.

Within a short time, William Aull realized that his wife's family could do a better job of raising Arthur than he could. The young boy lived with an aunt until about the time his father remarried in 1883. A year later, William Aull moved, with his new wife, son, and three stepchildren, from Illinois to Barton County, Missouri, where he purchased a farm in the Nashville Township. Although Arthur's stepmother, Nancy Jane, was not unkind to him, her own children came first. Years later Betty Aull White, the editor's daughter, recalled, "I asked him once, 'Was she good to you?' He said she wasn't mean. But she had a son from a former marriage. Dad said, 'When we'd come to town to buy clothes, she'd always buy him the best and me the cheapest. For our school lunches, I always had plenty in them, but his always had an apple or a surprise in it. And she always thought her son was very weak, so I had to do all the chores.' "[7]

As a teenager, Arthur Aull worked on his father's farm, dug coal, and helped build country bridges. He often worked as a hired hand on neighboring farms, where one day a "cultured older man" loaned him a book titled *A History of the World*. The fourteen-year-old Aull had worked in the fields all day, but he read the book all the way home, every step of the way, and far into the night. "It whetted his appetite for more," wrote his wife, Luanna, in 1961. "He didn't have access to a library, so every penny he earned went into books, that he read greedily." The boy's greatest delight was finding a book he had not previously read. Years later, he often told how enthralled he had been with a volume of Edward Gibbon's *Decline and Fall of the Roman Empire*.[8]

Aull attended the rural school in Nashville, Missouri, not far from his father's farm. His teacher, Thomas W. Martin, took a liking to the boy with an insatiable appetite for knowledge, and Martin would serve as Aull's mentor for the next two decades. Only nine years older than Aull, Martin also held teaching posts at Doylesport, North Star, and Liberal in Barton County before declaring himself a candidate for circuit clerk in 1890. Martin's campaign gave Aull his first taste of politics, and the future editor spent a good deal of time stumping for his friend in the western part of the county. One of Martin's former students at Doylesport, Walter Mayes, orated for him in the eastern half of the county. Although the two had never met, a rivalry developed between the two aspiring politicians. Martin was elected, and both hoped for the appointment as his deputy. The job went to Mayes, leaving Aull greatly disappointed.[9]

When Martin left the Nashville School, Aull had enrolled in the Fort Scott Normal School, a small college across the state line in Fort Scott, Kansas. There he studied history, language, and literature for two terms before taking his first teaching position at his old school in Nashville. Later, he moved a few miles north to the West Star School, where he taught orthography (spelling), history, grammar, geography, arithmetic, physiology, and language while studying law at night. Aull hoped to acquire enough knowledge to pass the Missouri bar examination in a few years and thus end his teaching career. Martin, after four years as county clerk, had been admitted to the bar to practice law without benefit of a law school education, and Aull dreamed of following in his footsteps.[10]

As a teacher, Aull had to spend a month every summer at the Lamar College renewing his teaching certificate. Founded in 1889, the college was an imposing two-story brick and stone building with a basement and a tower. It stood atop a hill overlooking the southeast part of Lamar, where students came from surrounding towns by horse and buggy. The landscaped grounds were shaded by majestic trees, a fitting place for Aull to meet the woman who would become his wife in the summer of 1895.[11]

Luanna Belle Turnbull, born in Lewis, Iowa, on April 6, 1873, had lived on the High Plains frontier of western Nebraska before moving with her family to Lamar at the age of fifteen. Her father, Oliver Turnbull, a cheerful man despite enduring a severe case of asthma throughout his life, taught his nine children to keep a positive outlook on life. A farmer by trade, he was used to hardships. Luanna's family had lived in a sod house near the Platte River in western Nebraska, where conditions were harsh.[12]

The Turnbulls survived the blizzard of 1888, which struck on a January morning after Luanna and her siblings of school age had been driven to the one-room schoolhouse on the prairie by their father. By noon, the snowfall was so heavy that when the teacher went out for coal he became lost only a hundred feet away and had to rely on the voices of the playing children to guide him back. The students were kept in the schoolhouse overnight by the teacher, who refused to allow any of them to attempt to reach their homes. The anxious families found their children secure the next morning. Others were not as fortunate, however. A nearby schoolma'am lost a hand to frostbite when she tried to make it home, lost her way, and spent the night in a haystack. Across the state, the blizzard resulted in an estimated one hundred to one thousand deaths.[13] Seeking a warmer climate, the Turnbulls moved to Lamar that fall.

In Luanna Turnbull, Aull discovered someone who shared his zest for life and his love of literature. He also took a liking to her family, something that had been lacking in his life since the death of his mother. The two wanted to marry, but their precarious teaching situations prevented a union from taking place immediately. Betty Aull White recalled:

> Dad told her, "We'll get married if I get the Nashville school," the highest-paying school in the district. But they came to Mamma and offered it to her. She said, "Well, I don't think I'll take it. If I don't take it, whom will you hire?" They named somebody else, and it wasn't Dad.
>
> She and Dad were such different teachers. If Dad had a very brilliant child in his class, that boy almost got a college education. My mother would work with the stupid more than the brilliant. That's why she might have been preferred.[14]

Aull encouraged Luanna to accept the Nashville position; he had been offered the superintendency at nearby Mindenmines. They were married by a justice of the peace on March 22, 1896, at Nashville. A daughter, Madeleine, was born to the couple eight months later, on November 20, at their home in Mindenmines.

Even on both their salaries, the Aulls struggled to make ends meet. They made considerably less than the fifty dollars a month the top teachers earned. To make matters worse, teaching didn't particularly stimulate Arthur Aull. He wanted to write more than anything else. Aull began to pursue his interest in politics again, speaking at numerous Free Silver meetings throughout Barton County in the summer and fall of 1896. He gained the favor of the local Democratic Party, which placed him on the ticket as its candidate for county surveyor. Aull defeated Republican Albert Chancellor by some eight hundred votes on November 3, two weeks shy of his twenty-fourth birthday.[15] Thomas Martin won his race for state representative, and Douglas Inglish, another Aull ally, was elected county treasurer.

PURCHASE OF THE *LAMAR DEMOCRAT*

For three years, Aull taught school and served as county surveyor from his home in Mindenmines. Still, he yearned for something more. One evening in 1899, after picking up surveying orders in Lamar, he rushed home to his wife with some exciting news: the *Democrat* was for sale again. Luanna Aull was enthusiastic but skeptical. The price was six thousand dollars, high by contemporary standards. In comparison, William Allen White had paid three thousand dollars for the *Emporia* (Kansas) *Gazette* four years earlier, and even that price was considered excessive. The fact that the *Democrat* had gone through three owners in the last five years made its purchase even riskier. "The paper hadn't been doing too well, as we knew, but we were both young with high hopes and confidence in his ability," Luanna Aull recollected in 1957.[16]

Still, the young teacher needed more than his wife's confidence to acquire the *Democrat*. Aull's friends from the local Democratic Party—namely Martin, Inglish, and John Pahlow—talked him into borrowing the six thousand dollars. He turned to George Crenshaw, president of the C. H. Brown Banking Company in Lamar, who was regarded as the "business guide and father confessor of half the men in the county." As he had done with hundreds of other promising entrepreneurs, Crenshaw backed Aull to the limit. "He got the money and came back walking on air," Luanna Aull recalled.[17]

Despite his lack of journalistic training, Aull fit the bill of a country editor. Ed Howe, editor of the *Atchison* (Kansas) *Globe,* theorized for *Century* magazine in 1891 that four groups of men generally owned country papers: farmers' sons, teachers, unsuccessful lawyers, and "professional printers." Aull qualified under the first two categories, and he had dreamed of becoming a lawyer. Printing, though, didn't interest him in the least. It was once pointed out that he couldn't set a lick of type, even if the front page depended on it. But what he lacked in technological savvy, Aull made up for with his writing ability. It was his command of the English language and his knack for turning a phrase that sold Martin, his former teacher, on his ability to take over the *Democrat.* In response to the many skeptics in town, Martin replied that Aull would become the best editor Lamar ever had.[18]

Fortunately for the neophyte editor and publisher, the *Democrat* employed George and Peggy Ward as a foreman/printer and typesetter, respectively, when he assumed control of the paper in August 1900. They took full charge of the mechanical end, allowing Aull to concentrate on his writing. Aull and George Ward, the grandson and namesake of Lamar's founding father, soon came to view each other as brothers. A deep affection and admiration developed between the two men and their families, and the Aulls never hesitated to credit the Wards for the success of the *Democrat* in the early days.[19]

Their financial situation was perilous at best when Aull took over the paper. Apprehensive about carving out a living and paying the interest on the six-thousand-dollar loan, the Aulls decided that Luanna would assume Arthur's teaching position at Mindenmines. This meant the temporary separation of the young family, however. Daughter Madeleine, not quite four, was placed in the care of Luanna's father and sisters in Lamar. Unable to bear the separation, Luanna resigned her position over the Christmas holidays in 1900, and the family "roughed it out."[20]

The loss of his wife's income created a serious cash flow problem for the fledgling editor. Aull was wary of offending delinquent subscribers and advertisers and preferred to spend his time chasing down stories rather than debtors. An even greater concern was the condition of his "rheumatic typesetter" and "battered handpress." He went back to Crenshaw, and the two devised a plan where Aull would sell stock in the *Democrat* to finance the purchase of new equipment. His Democratic friends—again Martin, Inglish, and Pahlow—were the primary investors. Crenshaw also informed Aull that the bank would cover all his debts and that he was not to let any bills go unpaid.[21]

LAMAR AND BARTON COUNTY

Lamar, 120 miles due south of Kansas City, was a shady county-seat town of 2,700 when Aull purchased the *Democrat*. The town was anything but quiet, though. It provided enough political maneuvering, petty rivalries and jealousies, and moral transgressions that the editor had little problem keeping his readers enthralled for nearly fifty years. Once described by a writer as "a Democratic island in the sea of Southwest Missouri Republicanism," the town's favorite pastime consisted of forming political rings and machines that endeavored to control both parties' tickets and committees.[22] Appropriately, Harry S. Truman was born in Lamar in 1884. But long before Truman elevated the town into the national spotlight, Lamar carried enough political clout to be visited by William Jennings Bryan in 1904 and Theodore Roosevelt in 1912.

The town was even named for a politician, Maribeau Bonaparte Lamar, a hero of the Texas Revolution and the Mexican War and the second president of the Republic of Texas. First settled in 1852, the town, like its namesake, possessed a rich history. William Quantrill, the notorious guerrilla chief, raided the village twice, in 1862 and 1864. In 1863, unidentified raiders burned the courthouse and most of the other buildings on the square.[23] Lamar incorporated as a town early in 1870 and hired Wyatt Earp, then only twenty-one, as its first constable. He stayed less than a year, leaving soon after his wife died of typhoid fever.

Lamar, with its imposing town square and broad streets, served as the trade center of Barton County. The centerpiece of the square was a three-story county courthouse, constructed of red brick and Barton County sandstone in 1889 to replace the one burned during the Civil War. Immediately upon the completion of the courthouse, the *Democrat* moved into the west half of the basement, a splendid spot from which to cover the county's news. The paper rented the space from the county court until 1909, when the newly elected Republican court demanded that Aull vacate the premises.[24]

Barton County, where many of the paper's rural subscribers resided, was the leading coal producer in the state. In the western part of the

county, near the Kansas state line, coal mining camps dotted the landscape. Two or three camps had populations of more than a thousand. In
Mindenmines, where Aull taught school before buying the *Democrat,*
the miners' monthly payroll sometimes reached one hundred thousand
dollars. The coal business, though, turned out to be more detrimental
than beneficial to the county in the long run. The strip-pit mining disfigured and damaged the land. Most of the coal near the surface had
been removed by 1910, leading to the eventual unemployment of many
of the miners. Aull took a drive through several of the old mining camps
one Sunday in June 1911 and was struck by the "misery, discontent,
and hideous poverty" left by the decline of the coal industry.[25]

Except for the mining district, Barton County was sparsely populated. Vast sections of virgin prairie and dense wooded areas gave parts
of it a wildernesslike atmosphere. The county led the state in prairie hay
production and was among the leaders in poultry farming. It was served
by two railroads, the north-south Missouri-Pacific and the east-west St.
Louis and San Francisco, which crossed in Lamar. Muddy Creek, which
followed a thirty-mile course through Barton County, along with Horse
Creek to the north, allegedly provided numerous hideouts to the James
and Dalton gangs in the late nineteenth century and to Pretty Boy
Floyd years later.[26]

2

N E W S P A P E R W A R

Fifty years ago, a newspaper was very largely a political institution. Today, it is a business affair almost pure and simple. That's why the political paper is pushed off the map. Any paper that depends on politics is bound to go broke.

—*Arthur Aull, January 15, 1925*

At the turn of the century, Lamar, Missouri, was a three-newspaper town. The weekly *Republican,* established in 1867; the weekly *Democrat,* established in 1870; and the daily *Leader,* a Populist-turned-Democratic paper established in 1890, were purely political organs. A fourth paper, the Republican weekly *Sentinel,* would join the mix in 1903.

The *Democrat* and the *Leader* boasted an inherent advantage in a town that had been controlled by the Democratic Party since its establishment. In the 1860 presidential election, Abraham Lincoln received only 9 percent of the vote in Barton County. Word of Lincoln's election reportedly triggered brawls in the streets and saloons of Lamar and secret meetings among citizens in neighboring settlements.[1]

When twenty-seven-year-old Arthur Aull assumed control of the *Democrat* with the August 9, 1900, issue, he made it clear that his primary goal was to disseminate the views of the Democratic Party as the paper had always done. He declared in his salutatory editorial that his policy would be "to continue to proclaim the tenets" advocated by Thomas Jefferson,

Andrew Jackson, and William Jennings Bryan, the "great champions of the rights of the people." Aull also pledged his support to the local Democratic ticket, "from representative to coroner," and vowed to make the *Democrat* a "truly good newspaper and a sound party organ."[2]

Most country editors of this era functioned as politicians to some degree. They were expected to advocate the election of the straight party ticket, keep their readers apprised of what was happening in county politics, and make periodic attacks on the opposing political party and newspaper. In return, the elected officials of their party rewarded them with the county legal notices and political printing. Editors were allowed to bill at the maximum rate for legal advertising, often five times as much as other county newspapers would have charged.

A country newspaper's income was derived from five sources: subscriptions, job printing, legal advertising, local advertising, and regional and national advertising. Legal advertising was the most lucrative, and as a result, the competition for it was often cutthroat. Most small towns had at least two newspapers, some three or four, due to the fact that anybody could start one and every political faction had to have one. Partisan newspapers were, as a rule, unrestrained in Aull's early days due to the nature of party politics of the time. Nearly every newspaper was "married" to a party, and nearly all news was political; a newspaper had little to publish unless it was fighting the cause of its controlling party. Its reward was the ample legal advertising safeguarded by the party's elected officials.[3]

A conflict over political windfalls in 1901 triggered a ferocious newspaper war between the *Republican,* the *Democrat,* and the *Leader.* Feuds between country editors were commonplace around the turn of the century, but few were as malicious as this one. William Allen White, the embodiment of the small-town newspaperman, was caught up in a newspaper war shortly after his purchase of the *Emporia* (Kansas) *Gazette* in 1895. White's run-in was with a fellow Republican editor in Emporia over the city printing contract.[4] But whereas White, the newcomer, later reached an agreement with his more-established adversary to split the printing fees equally, Aull accepted no quarter in his feud with Arthur Rozelle, editor of the *Leader,* and John McCreary, editor of the *Republican.*

The exchanges between Aull and Rozelle became so malicious that blistering summer of 1901 that criminal libel suits eventually were filed against all three Lamar editors by the Barton County prosecuting attorney. Envious of the substantial legal advertising the *Democrat* received, Rozelle and McCreary conspired to seize a portion of it for themselves. They assailed the young editor, thinking his takeover of the *Democrat* was the perfect time to make inroads into its public patronage. Aull, however, met the challenge and launched his own vicious attack against the two editors. McCreary soon found that he couldn't stomach such a controversy and pulled the *Republican* out.

Although no fisticuffs were exchanged between Aull and Rozelle, their verbal face-off was as nasty as newspaper wars get. After the criminal libel charges were filed against the three editors, Rozelle expected to be vindicated when all the details of Aull's alleged "printing steal" were made known. Instead, as reported by the *Carthage* (Missouri) *Evening Press,* "Rozelle got such a showing up in court that he doubtless wishes he had never mentioned the subject of libel."[5] The trial attracted the attention of the entire state and did as much as anything else to spring Aull to fame in Missouri.

Arthur Rozelle would have been a formidable adversary for an experienced newspaperman, let alone a newly minted one. An organizer of the People's Party in Missouri, Rozelle had been elected state chairman of the Populists in 1894 and reelected in 1896. When the new party began to divide over the issue of fusing with the Democrats or maintaining a separate organization, Rozelle led his element of the Populists into the Democratic Party.[6] In recognition of his services to the Democrats in the 1896 campaign, he was appointed state labor commissioner the following year by Governor Lon Stephens. The forty-one-year-old Rozelle was also a seasoned newspaperman who had established papers at Coin, Iowa, and Tarkio, Missouri, before coming to Lamar in 1895. He purchased the *Lamar Industrial Union,* a Farm and Labor Union paper, and soon converted it to a daily named the *Lamar Leader.*

A FUROR OVER POLITICAL PATRONAGE

After his purchase of the *Democrat* in 1900, Aull waited but a week before launching his first attack against the *Republican,* claiming that he would show the falsity of the newspaper's recent corruption charges against Democratic officials in Barton County. The new publisher wrote: "In short we believe that it is time to call a halt, turn the light on these self-styled 'purifiers,' and meet them in the arena which they, themselves, have entered."[7] Aull subsequently denounced the Barton County sheriff and county clerk, both Republicans, for placing their legal notices in the *Republican* at double the rate the *Democrat* would have charged.

As the official organ of the Barton County Democratic Party, the *Democrat* received nearly all of its job printing. The *Leader,* one of three other Democratic newspapers in the county, printed only the legal notices of the Populist circuit clerk and probate judge. With the November 1900 election of a Democratic sheriff, John Harlow, the *Republican*'s public printing was limited to that of the county clerk.

Both the *Leader* and the *Republican* criticized the Democratic county court for failing to accept sealed bids on the publication of its financial statement. Soon after Aull's takeover of the *Democrat,* the *Leader* offered to print the court's statement for twenty cents per square—twenty cents per square less than the *Democrat* was charging.[8] The county court maintained that it was not compelled to seek bids, that "under the law it had a right to let the printing to whomever it chose, and that this printing in common with all other of the county patronage should be let to the official organ of the party in power." The *Democrat* ultimately published the 1901 financial statement of the county court at nineteen and one-half cents per square, which Aull declared was "cheaper than ever before in the history of the county, and cheaper than the *Leader* itself signified its willingness to publish it."[9]

In the summer of 1901, the *Republican* initiated an investigation of the *Democrat*'s public printing that eventually led to the county filing criminal libel charges against all three Lamar newspapers for flagrantly disturbing the community peace. The *Republican* initially charged the *Democrat* with defrauding the county's taxpayers by printing excessive deed blanks for Sheriff John Harlow and Charles Glenn, recorder of deeds, and charging exorbitant prices. Aull accused the newspaper of "mere jealousy" of the *Democrat,* and said if the *Republican*'s real desire was to serve the taxpayers as purported, it should allow the *Democrat* to take over the county clerk's printing at half the price charged by the *Republican.* "We don't know what its prices have been, but we are perfectly willing to risk all of that, in order to give this virtuous, immaculate sheet an opportunity to prove its love for the taxpayers," Aull wrote in July 1901.[10]

EDITORS EXCHANGE ACCUSATIONS

The *Leader* then charged the *Democrat* with "high handed robbery" following the *Republican* exposé and a further examination of the records. Arthur Rozelle, editor of the *Leader*, alleged:

> Barton County has been defrauded. The professed "official organ" is the perpetrator of this fraud. Not satisfied with charging the county three prices for printing, it makes a charge and collects at least seventy dollars for work that was never done. The concern or individual who will perpetrate such a fraud is no better than a thief and ought to be prosecuted for obtaining money under false pretenses.[11]

The *Leader* alleged that the *Democrat* printed one thousand assessor's blanks for Glenn, the recorder of deeds, but charged for four jobs at the "enormous rate" of fifty dollars. The *Democrat,* according to the *Leader,* then printed another thousand of the blanks and charged thirty-five dollars for the paper and press work. The *Democrat* also charged thirty-five dollars for one thousand legal forms and another thirty-five dollars for certificates, the latter two charges "being entirely fictitious." Rozelle, who urged the county court to make the "thief disgorge," said "the trouble with the 'great' editor of the 'organ' is, he imagines he is the Democratic party of Barton county, when figuratively speaking, he is only the little dog under the wagon."[12]

Aull, while not denying the *Leader*'s allegations except to say the sheriff's deeds usually were needed in great quantity, attempted to portray the *Leader* as assailing the character of Edwin L. Moore, Barton County prosecuting attorney, for approving the *Democrat*'s bill as the legal adviser to the court. "His public record is above reproach and the *Leader*'s implied attack upon him is not only without foundation, but it shows that the chief reason . . . is to attack democratic officials." Aull also shouted that a "pie combination" existed between Rozelle and the *Republican*'s John McCreary—that the two editors had combined to attack Barton County Democratic officials in an attempt to "route the regular democracy and divide the pie between them."[13]

The *Leader*'s printing prices and subscription rate were questioned by Aull as well. He cited its forty-five-dollar charge for printing a pamphlet containing the January 1901 court docket and said the *Democrat* could print the same document for twenty dollars and not lose any money. He

also volunteered to print the legal notices of the circuit clerk and probate judge at half the price the *Leader* had been charging. And of the
Leader and its dollar-per-year subscription rate, Aull said:

> It contains a few antiquated newspaper clippings, a lot of patent
> medicine ads, a few locals, an occasional "roast" on some citizen, and
> four pages of boiler plate. The *St. Louis Republic* is issued twice a week;
> each issue contains more original news matter than the *Leader* will
> contain in forty years, and it costs only a dollar a year. The *Kansas City
> Star* issues a weekly edition that contains more original matter in one
> issue than the editor of the *Leader* has ever written, and it can be got-
> ten for twenty-five cents a year.[14]

Aull, however, saved most of his venom for Rozelle himself. Under
the headline "Wolf in Sheep's Clothing," Aull on August 1, 1901, detailed how Rozelle had been posing as a friend and champion of the taxpayers when, in effect, he was swindling them by publishing the probate
docket at five times the necessary cost. Aull assailed his counterpart for
asking to print the county court's financial statement at twenty cents
per square yet charging the probate judge one dollar per square:

> Isn't that devotion to the taxpayers with double distilled
> vengeance? Are the people of Barton county going to be deceived by
> such bold pretense and shameless hypocrisy? Does this scurrilous sheet
> and the Judas Iscariot that edits it, believe that they can pose as friends
> of the people and taxpayers, when according to their own testimony
> they rob them to the tune of five and six hundred percent? No one but
> a confirmed political blackmailer and a hopelessly hardened boodler
> would ever think of such nonsense.[15]

Aull also brought up Rozelle's political record, claiming that he sold
out the Populist Party and that the *Leader* had advocated the defeat of
the Democratic Party in the 1896 election. Rozelle "looted and cheated
and robbed and betrayed, until he was practically kicked out; then
he came down here and began to pose as a friend of the taxpayers. Isn't
that a *democratic* (?) [Aull's italics] record for you?" Aull then challenged
Rozelle to allow a reputable citizen to examine the *Leader's* back issues
to reveal exactly what the newspaper had printed about the 1896
Democratic ticket; Rozelle replied that Aull himself was welcome to in-
spect the files to his heart's content. He wrote that if Aull "finds a line

by the present editor advising populists to fuse with the Republicans in this county or elsewhere, we will forfeit more than he 'collected' from the county treasury for printing that was never done."[16]

The day after Aull's "Wolf in Sheep's Clothing" exposé, Rozelle accused the *Democrat*'s editor of "getting slightly personal" and said it was a game "that more than one can play at." He asked Aull to stop his "coarse billingsgate and personal abuse" long enough to explain why he had charged $50 for the first one thousand assessor's blanks and $105 for the second thousand, which were not even bound.[17] Announcing that the *Leader*'s investigation was complete, Rozelle urged the rank and file of the Barton County Democratic Party to do their duty and demand that the county court expunge its mistake of allowing the *Democrat*'s fraudulent printing bills.

What small measure of civility Aull and Rozelle had shown one another earlier soon vanished. Rozelle's attacks, initially not as blistering and personal as Aull's, quickly matched them in both intensity and dastardliness. "The skunk who inhabits the cellar seems to be suffering with a bad case of rabies," he wrote, referring to Aull's office in the basement of the Barton County courthouse. He even attempted to explain the rationale behind Aull's "extortion" of money from the county treasury: "Sonny's raven locks hadn't been trimmed in a twelve month and he needed some pocket change, and besides the rent hadn't been paid for almost a year and the interest was past due on the mortgage and— well cash was needed, so more deeds were printed by 1500 than was ordered and the bill swelled to $100 for deeds."[18]

Rozelle pointed out that Aull had called him "Judas Iscariot" forty-five times, a "liar" sixty-two times, a "hypocrit" [*sic*] twenty-one times, and a "harlot" twenty-six times. As a small measure of revenge, he pointed out that Aull's subscription to the *Leader* had gone unpaid for several years. "Not even a cent of his ill gotten gains from the county has been applied on this account."[19]

As the war between the two editors raged, Barton County and most of the Corn Belt suffered from such a severe drought that Governor Alexander Dockery seriously considered issuing an edict that the state's citizenry assemble to pray for rain. Temperatures ranged from 105 to 115 degrees in Barton County. The corn crop was a total failure and water for livestock became increasingly scarce. The situation wasn't any more tolerable in Lamar, causing a newspaper in an adjoining county to declare that the town was "short on ice and long on hot air." The *Jasper*

County (Missouri) *Democrat* further commented on the "sizzling" controversy between Aull and Rozelle: "Citizens stand round with a bucket of water in each hand to extinguish the blazes everywhere originating from spontaneous combustion. The situation forcibly reminds visitors of Satan's fiery furnace when his majesty's furies are wearied."[20]

The *Lamar Republican,* which had launched the investigation into the *Democrat's* public printing, now tried to back out of the newspaper war. Its only comment on the situation, surprisingly, was to fault Rozelle for his conduct: "Neighbor Rozelle seems to be a misfit as a Democratic editor. The idea of a Democratic editor exposing in the columns of his paper the boodling of Democratic officials and the thefts of Democratic pie-grabbers is something new and unheard of in Democratic journalism. The *Leader* will have to recant or be disciplined for conduct unbecoming a Democratic paper." The *Republican* may have abandoned its attack on Aull and the *Democrat* for fear of libel charges. Aull, knowing there was no turning back on his part or Rozelle's, hinted at what was to come: "Judas, if you're not a boodler, a betrayer, a sandbagger and a thief, *you've* [Aull's italics] got an excellent opportunity for a libel suit."[21] That comment on August 8, 1901, marked his first anniversary as editor of the *Democrat,* a tumultuous year by any standard.

Rozelle received more ammunition to use against Aull upon the release of the report of a committee appointed by the county court to examine the records of officials whose successors were elected in November 1900. Aull, who served as county surveyor and bridge commissioner before his purchase of the *Democrat,* was included in the August 7, 1901, report. The nonpartisan committee found that Aull, as bridge commissioner, had twice presented claims for payment for work done on June 2 and June 4, 1900. The committee also noted that as surveyor, Aull had recorded his bond in the county clerk's office when, by law, it was to have been registered in the recorder of deeds' office. Rozelle showed remarkable restraint editorially, saying only in the August 16 *Leader,* "Our readers can draw their own conclusions."[22]

Aull also publicized the results of the committee's investigation, but offered no defense of its finding pertaining to him. Instead, he focused on the $175 former Sheriff J. P. Phillips, a Republican, owed the county for overcharges. Aull praised the work of the county treasurer, public administrator, and coroner, all Democrats, and said the report provided "additional evidence that the local democracy can be trusted by the people, and that Barton county democrats, when they adhere strictly to their party ticket are not only strengthening their party, but they are serving the best interests of the people."[23]

A MYSTERIOUS LETTER TO THE EDITOR

The next development in the newspaper war was the front-page publication of an anonymous letter to the editor in the *Leader*'s Saturday evening edition of August 17, 1901. Spanning a third of the page, the letter from "A Lifelong Democrat" most likely was written by Rozelle, since it closely resembled his previous comments about the editor of the *Democrat*. The letter, for example, referred to Aull as "the owl eyed, raven locked pencil pusher," descriptions Rozelle had used before. The writer's tone, style, and vocabulary also matched that of Rozelle:

> His rottenness smells to high heaven. The readers of his puerile productions which he fondly imagines the people will call editorials, were they not acquainted with his iniquitous record, might be inveigled into believing him one of the long departed saints, returned to mother earth for the purpose of reclaiming the world from its sin; but too well they know his shady record to be misled by his weak attempts at bombast, and his scurrilous and vituperative attacks on the editor of the *Leader*. His peregrinations around town remind one of a boy with his first pair of boots. He imagines himself to be the cynosure of all eyes, not realizing that the people regard him as an egregious ass.[24]

Aull immediately branded it a "fake" letter, demanding that Rozelle reveal the identity of the writer. "If he cannot produce the name of the man who wrote the article every democrat in Barton County will know that A. Rozelle is an open and notorious liar and a blackmailer." Rozelle's response was that the writer was "one of the best known Democrats of Barton county" and "a man of unblemished reputation, who stands high in Democratic councils." And the reason for not divulging his name? "When a skunk has his gun cocked, no man will willingly go within his range."[25]

Meanwhile, Rozelle challenged Aull to produce any evidence that as state chairman of the Populist Party he had received financial support from the chairman of the Republican state committee or fifteen hundred dollars from the Democratic Party in the 1896 election. Rozelle proposed that Aull select an impartial committee of three Democrats to procure any evidence and determine if his charges were true. If they were, Rozelle said he would pay the costs of the investigation and one hundred dollars to a worthy charity, provided that Aull "show equal candor and ask for an investigation of his 'printing steal' from Barton county." Aull dismissed Rozelle's offer as "the purest buncombe," because such a committee would have no power to compel potential witnesses to testify.[26]

LIBEL CHARGES ARE FILED

As the summer of 1901 ended, Edwin Moore, the prosecuting attorney of Barton County, declined an appointment by the county court to a committee charged with determining whether Aull indeed had obtained money by false pretense. When the court failed to pursue such an investigation, Moore filed criminal libel suits in circuit court against all three Lamar editors for flagrantly disturbing the peace and good order of the community. Rozelle and McCreary were charged with publishing and circulating a libel against Aull; Aull was accused of uttering and publishing a libel against Rozelle.

Criminal libel suits, almost unheard of today, were fairly common in the late nineteenth and early twentieth centuries due to the excesses of political party journalism. According to an 1893 New York court, "A criminal libel is prosecuted in the name of the people, not for the purpose of redressing an injury done to an individual, but is so prosecuted and punished as a crime, for the reason that it tends to disturb the public peace and repose." Criminal libel differed from civic libel in that the publisher was punished by fine or imprisonment for the crime of publishing defamatory words, whereas in civic libel the person whose reputation was defamed was given compensatory damages.[27]

On Tuesday morning, September 17, the three editors appeared in court and were asked by Judge H. C. Timmonds if they were prepared for trial. Attorneys for Rozelle and McCreary said their clients were ready as soon as witnesses could be summoned; Aull's attorney, however, asked for a continuance. Timmonds then postponed the cases to the next term of the circuit court and released the newspapermen on their own recognizance after each posted one hundred dollars. Rozelle couldn't resist taking one last jab at Aull, observing: "It is a fact, perhaps worthy of note, that when the wholesale grist of libel cases were called in court Tuesday morning, the editor of the *Leader* promptly answered through, his attorney, 'ready for trial.' The *Leader* is always willing to back up every allegation that it publishes, or stand the consequences."[28]

FORMER GOVERNOR ENTERS THE FRAY

Aull received a boost from an unexpected source just three days after his court appearance. Former Governor Lon Stephens, who had named Rozelle state labor commissioner in 1897, attacked the *Leader* editor in his weekly newspaper column, "Sharps and Flats," in the *Boonville* (Missouri) *Weekly Advertiser*. Stephens, claiming the appointment was made because of his own "stupidity and credulity," bashed Rozelle for suing a "brother editor" for libel. Stephens went on to say, "Just when and where the ingrate and flannel-mouthed agitator will break loose next, is a problem only a prophet can solve."[29] Aull delighted in reproducing Stephens's column in the *Democrat*.

Rozelle, not entirely sure of the reprint's authenticity, nevertheless took the opportunity to blast the "ex-gubernatorial accident." He wrote: "This outbreak of the Ex-Governor is somewhat unexpected, but it is the unexpected that always happens in his case. As Artemus Ward would say, he is a most 'amoosin little cuss,' but just what his motive is in poking his proboscis into our business at such long range, we are unable to say." In addition, Rozelle claimed that Stephens's account of him suing Aull for libel was "a lie," that the lawsuit was initiated by Prosecutor Moore without Rozelle's knowledge.[30]

Stephens returned the fire from Boonville, saying Rozelle's reply in the *Leader* guaranteed him a job of cleaning spittoons at the next session of the Missouri House of Representatives. And "if he takes his pen in hand two or three more times, when inspiration comes to him, he will more than likely be given a guardship on the walls of the state prison," Stephens added.[31]

On January 1, 1902, shortly before the libel trial opened, Rozelle sold the *Leader* to Prosecuting Attorney Moore and William Warner and moved thirty miles south to Webb City, Missouri. There he assumed ownership and management of the *Webb City Register*.

THE STATE V. ARTHUR AULL

The trial of the *State of Missouri v. Arthur Aull* began in circuit court on Thursday morning, January 23, 1902, with the selection of the jury. Moore, assisted by John Cole, a partner in his law firm, represented the state, while B. G. Thurman and Thomas W. Martin made up Aull's defense team. Moore, first elected Barton County prosecuting attorney in 1894 at the age of twenty-four, would go on to serve two terms as a state representative and two terms as a state senator. He was a formidable adversary, but Aull's attorneys were craftier and more case-hardened. Thurman was a former state senator, a two-term prosecuting attorney of neighboring Dade County, and a newspaper editor and publisher for three years. Martin had been Democratic floor leader and chairman of the committee on criminal jurisprudence in the Missouri House of Representatives. He was also Aull's old schoolteacher and one of the *Democrat*'s major stockholders.

The entire morning was spent selecting the jury. Judge Timmonds ordered Sheriff Harlow to impanel two additional jurors to complete the panel of twenty, so that each side would be able to strike four. The selections were made by noon, and the court took a ninety-minute recess.

When the trial resumed, Moore laid out the state's case in his opening statement. The state, he said, based its prosecution on the following paragraph published in the *Democrat* on August 15, 1901: "Judas is giving the county court yards and yards of advice. The court must appreciate this. Honest men enjoy being told their duty by a thief, a boodler and a betrayer."[32]

Aull's attorneys had crafted a three-pronged defense that Martin unfolded in his opening statement. Their first argument was that Aull and Rozelle simply were embroiled in a newspaper controversy, that the public understood that the denunciations by the editors were "mere epithets." Next, Martin pointed out that Rozelle had called Aull a "thief" and a "boodler" before Aull had published the alleged libelous paragraph about the *Leader*'s editor. Finally, Martin said Aull's defense was truth, that they would be able to prove that Rozelle had violated the state constitution and illegally received money from the state.[33]

The first witness Moore called was W. H. Callahan, a justice of the peace. As a reader of the *Democrat,* Callahan testified about the harm done to society and the peace that had been breached. The state summoned four other witnesses and rested its case Thursday evening after having presented all its evidence in half a day.[34]

The editor of the *Democrat* took the stand Friday morning. He was asked by Thurman, "Under what circumstances did you make the publication," referring to the August 15 paragraph.[35] Cole objected for the state, claiming that the motives and intentions of the defendant were inadmissible. Judge Timmonds excused the jury as Thurman and Cole engaged in a lengthy argument that continued until nearly 12:30. An hour later, Timmonds dealt a serious blow to Aull's side with the announcement that he had sustained the state's objection. Aull's testimony continued, but all the questions put to him by his attorneys were objected to by Moore and Cole.

Timmonds further weakened Aull's case by not allowing the testimony of former Governor Stephens, who was at the trial along with Secretary of State Sam B. Cook, State Auditor Albert O. Allen, and James M. Seibert, former state auditor and state treasurer. Timmonds did permit Allen and Matt Carroll, chief clerk under Rozelle in the labor commissioner's office, to take the stand in Aull's behalf. Once Rozelle's protégé, Carroll now was his bitter enemy. Six years earlier, Rozelle had loaned him money to pay off a mortgage and move his family from Springfield, Missouri, to Lamar. The loan went unpaid, and Rozelle recently had won a judgment in a Jefferson City court. Aull had gone to Jefferson City himself in August 1901 to seek a written statement from Carroll about Rozelle's character. When Aull failed to use anything from Carroll in the *Democrat,* Rozelle chortled: "Now then, why didn't he publish it? The fact is, he is ashamed to do so. The source is too offensive. The name of M. V. Carroll is a stench in the nostrils of all decent fairminded people, here and elsewhere throughout the state."[36]

With the testimonies of Carroll and Allen, Aull's attorneys hoped to prove that Rozelle as labor commissioner had fraudulently procured money from the state. Moore and Cole objected to nearly every item of evidence brought forth; the objections were sustained. With that, the defense rested its case Friday evening.[37]

The courtroom was packed Saturday morning when all four attorneys made closing remarks. Moore spoke first, followed by Thurman, Martin, and Cole. According to trial coverage in the *Lamar Republican,* "These speeches abounded in irony and cutting sarcasm. At times they became quite bitter and very frequently the attorney addressing the jury was interrupted by an objection from counsel on the other side to some statement or allusion that had been made."[38]

Thurman and Martin blasted away at Moore, in particular, in urging acquittal for their client. They questioned the young prosecutor's motives for bringing Aull to trial in the first place and pointed out the bizarre conditions surrounding the case. Aull wrote later that Thurman's thirty-minute speech "made a profound impression, both upon the jury and the audience. It was probably never equaled, certainly never excelled in a Barton county courtroom."[39]

Aull's fate was put in the hands of the jury at three o'clock Saturday afternoon. The jury deliberated three hours without making a decision, then Timmonds dismissed it until Monday. After convening for slightly more than an hour Monday morning, the jury returned at 10:30 A.M. with a verdict of not guilty. The courtroom was nearly empty at the time, as it was expected that a decision would not come until later in the day. Aull, working in the *Democrat* office when the news came, quickly wrote an editorial in which he first saluted the jury: "The high character of the twelve gentlemen who sat in the trial, for integrity, and for sterling manhood renders the verdict all the more gratifying to the defendant and to his friends." He went on to applaud Thurman and Martin:

> The whole town resounds with plaudits for the attorneys for Mr. Aull. Their knowledge of the law, their eloquence, their matchless and unflinching courage in the face of difficulties which seemed almost insurmountable, on account of the rulings of the court, are subjects of almost universal discussion. No men ever made a braver fight; undismayed and undaunted, they stood forth boldly for the justice of their cause, winning in the end one of the most notable legal victories ever achieved in the whole history of Southwest Missouri.[40]

The *Leader*, not exactly gracious in defeat, tried to put its own spin on what had occurred in a same-day editorial: "At all events, the trial has demonstrated that it is impossible to convict a Democratic editor of libel in this county. At least it is no offense for him to publish that another man is a thief. Judge Timmonds was of the opinion in his instructions that it was, but the jury thought otherwise. We are glad to know this for our own good. We may have occasion to belabor some gentile in the days to come."[41]

In the case against Rozelle, the court held that the indictment was defective. The case against McCreary was postponed until the next term of the circuit court because the defendant was ill, then later dismissed.[42]

Was Aull guilty of defrauding the county treasury? A country newspaper should charge the maximum rates allowed by law for legal advertising, according to a 1906 speech he made to the Missouri Press Association in St. Louis. He said a newspaper makes a mistake by habitually cutting its prices to wrest printing accounts from its competitors because it was entitled to a legitimate profit from legal advertising.[43] Aull simply was practicing this idea in billing the circuit court and other officeholders at the legal rate of compensation. He never addressed Rozelle's other accusation that he charged seventy dollars for job printing never done.

Aull's victory in court was just as meaningful to his tell-all brand of journalism as it was to his reputation. Had he been found guilty of criminal libel, Aull faced imprisonment or a hefty fine, which certainly would have led to a chilling effect on his intrepid style of news coverage. Nearly thirty years would pass before Aull would run into another libel suit, and in the meantime, readers of the *Democrat* delighted in his unconventional approach to journalism.

THE NEXT TEN YEARS

Now that the issue had been settled, it was time to repair any damage done to the Democratic Party in Barton County. Aull expressed his hope that "a brighter and better day may dawn for the politics of Barton county and that such a remarkable spectacle may never again be thrust before the gaze of our people." The *Golden City Free Press,* a Republican newspaper in Barton County, was not as encouraging, saying the Lamar newspaper controversy had done more to disrupt the local Democratic Party than anything that had ever befallen county politics.[44]

As a direct result of the newspaper controversy, the Democratic county court decided to divide the printing of its financial statement between the *Democrat* and the *Leader.* The court was willing to pay forty-five cents per square—twenty-two and a half cents to the *Democrat* and twenty-two and a half cents to the *Leader.* This didn't satisfy the other Democratic newspapers in Barton County. The editor of the *Liberal Enterprise,* after its bid of twenty cents a square was ignored, said sarcastically, "[W]e thought there would be no harm in making an effort to save the taxpayers of the county some money."[45] Before the decade ended, the county court sought bids on all its printing, effectively wiping out any claims of partisan patronage.

Aull and Rozelle, now publishing the *Webb City Register,* continued to trade pot shots in the columns of their papers. Aull still was calling Rozelle "Judas Iscariot," alluding to his sellout of the Populist Party. But when Rozelle died of blood poisoning at his home in Webb City in 1912, the *Democrat*'s obituary offered no clue of the hatred between the two men. Though not lavishing praise on Rozelle, Aull did write, "He leaves behind him a prosperous newspaper and a considerable fortune."[46]

Aull also maintained a running feud with Moore, the prosecuting attorney, throughout the decade. His dislike for Moore boiled over in 1908 when Moore entered the race for state representative against Henry C. Chancellor, one of Aull's closest friends. Aull and others in the Barton County Democratic Party urged Moore to wait two years before running, but the attorney refused and went on to defeat Chancellor in the primary election and his Republican opponent that November.[47]

Aull blamed Moore for the Republicans winning the "best offices upon the ticket" in 1908 and the defeat of Democrat Smith Long in the Barton County treasurer's race, which he called a "palpable and undeniable conspiracy." Aull alleged that Moore had brought the entire Barton County Democratic ticket down with his talk of party corruption. "If Mr. Moore should be a candidate for something, and any one had the temerity to oppose him, he would no doubt, as he did this time, swear that every man of any prominence or activity, who supported his opponent, was a member of a notorious, corrupt, infamous gang," Aull claimed. Moore, never one to back down, replied with a seething letter to the editor. "In your disappointment over the election, your ancient grudge against me rises uppermost, and you therefore make me the target for your resentment," he wrote.[48]

Years later, the two came to value each other's friendship. They realized they held the same interests—history, poetry, literature, and Barton County politics—and developed a mutual respect. Moore became one of Aull's attorneys and helped defend him in a ten-thousand-dollar libel suit in the 1930s. He even went so far as to select the editor as one of his six honorary pallbearers prior to his death in 1942. And in his obituary of Moore, Aull described him as "unique, original, a landmark in Lamar for more than half a century."[49]

A CHANGE IN PHILOSOPHY

While not severing his ties to the local Democratic Party, Aull started moving the *Democrat* away from party control before the first decade of his ownership was over. An editor had an easier time soliciting subscriptions and serving the entire community when he wasn't regarded as an "organ grinder." Aull, a shrewd businessman above all else, expressed his newfound philosophy in 1908:

> So far as this paper is concerned, it is not greatly worried about politics, so if you want to spite it, choose some other way. We want to see the Democratic ticket successful, but we don't want to see it any worse than you do, if you're a good Democrat, and, seriously, its defeat won't hurt us much—only our feelings. . . .
>
> Point out to us a newspaper that has played the political game, good and strong, that hasn't come out [a] loser in the end, and we'll show you a white crow. . . . We want to run a Democratic paper, but above all we shall try to run a paper that gives every element in the community a decent and a fair consideration—the community is too small to do anything else. And, in conclusion let us say, that we have long since learned—we admit we didn't know it at first—that it is better, pleasanter, and more profitable, so far as the newspaper itself is concerned, to serve the whole public than to serve any set of men, any faction—or any one part of the people.[50]

Other country editors were also moving their papers from political dependence to independence. Declining political influence, coupled with an abundance of profitable national advertising, caused many to forsake their status as party organs. By 1925, the day of the partisan newspaper had passed, according to *Scribner's Magazine*. "Obviously, it is not good business to appeal to the members of only one party," the magazine observed. "Why should any publisher cut his possible circulation in half by continually publishing the ideas and principles of only one party?"[51]

Aull, who found the content of party newspapers tiresome and ineffectual, preferred to spend his newsgathering time looking for the sensational story that would appeal to readers of the *Democrat*. "It occurs to us," he wrote in 1922, "the stronger a paper goes in on politics, the less power it will exert. A newspaper makes its money, primarily, by printing such information, as the public likes best to read."[52]

3

ALL THE NEWS IS
FIT TO PRINT

> It would never do for Yours Truly to go to heaven. When they asked him to come over and listen to the angel choir, he'd be sure to say, "Nope, gotta get across and dig up something to keep the machine going, so the paper can get out." Then St. Peter'd grab him by the scruff of the neck, and say, "What! You don't mean to say you brought that dirty little pocket handkerchief Daily with you, do you!"
>
> —*Arthur Aull, June 7, 1923*

News of a sensational nature intrigued Arthur Aull. Even before launching his own newspapering career, he observed that papers employing the "new style of journalism" flourished because of their appeal to the masses. William Randolph Hearst's *New York Journal* and *Chicago American,* two of the leading practitioners of "yellow journalism," were luring readers and advertisers while their "staid, old-style competitors" struggled to stay afloat amid the depression of the 1890s. "A careful investigation of the matter thus leads one to conclude that the new style of journalism succeeds, largely because it meets the requirements of the people," Aull wrote shortly after his purchase of the *Lamar Democrat.*[1]

The newly minted editor immediately decided to apply the formula of the "yellow press" to his own paper. Although country folk were more likely than city dwellers to read a newspaper "through and through," they, too, yearned for the unusual and sensational.[2] And so,

stories of grisly accidents, murders, rapes, juvenile crime, suicides and
attempted suicides, and scandalous divorces became Aull's trademark.
But he embellished nearly all his sensational stories with a personal,
homespun flavor, and that is what caught the attention of the syndicated columnists, metropolitan press, and popular magazines toward
the latter part of his career.

For the most part, the *Lamar Democrat* was an uninteresting and
unimaginative newspaper before Aull took control in 1900. Much of
the content consisted of stale "boiler plate," ready-to-print miscellany
purchased from syndicates or supplied by advertisers. Business cards
from local professionals and merchants (including one from Arthur
Aull, county surveyor, in 1899), ads, long political articles, and an occasional treatise on the soil and climate of southwest Missouri rounded
out the four-page editions. Local news was almost nonexistent.

AN UNCONVENTIONAL APPROACH

Aull's sensationalistic approach flew in the face of conventional country journalism wisdom. Even the big-city papers that had given rise to
the "new journalism" had abandoned much of the practice by the end
of the first decade of the twentieth century.[3] Yet throughout his career
Aull followed the policy of printing anything that told of agony and
misfortune, for he believed that was what his readers wanted. He explained his theory in 1909:

> One of the unfortunate things about the newspaper business is the
> fact that the real, red-hot news, that the people really enjoy is the
> chronicle of some great and crushing misfortune. A man loses his
> business honor, a woman sinks into the mire of shame, some troubled
> soul seeks surcease from sorrow in a bullet or a dose of poison—these
> are a newspaper's most valuable assets—because they are the things
> about which people, above all other things, want.[4]

Authors of articles and handbooks about country journalism warned
against the publication of crime and scandal, however. Charles Moreau
Harger, writing in the *Atlantic Monthly* in 1907, claimed that while a
country editor might be eager to print all the news of his community,
he seldom did in the interest of his own safety:

So the country editor leaves out certain good things and certain bad things for the very simple reason that the persons most interested are close at hand and can find the individual responsible for the statements. He becomes wise in his generation and avoids chastisement and libel suits. He finds that there is no lasting regard in a sneer, no satisfaction in gratifying the impulse to say things that bring tears to women's eyes, nothing to gloat over in opening a wound in a man's heart. If he does not learn this as he grows older in the service, he is a poor country editor.[5]

Charles Laurel Allen, assistant dean and director of research at the Medill School of Journalism at Northwestern University, urged country editors in 1928 to publish news only of a "constructive nature" since they were dealing with the rural community rather than city dwellers. Allen's logic followed that in the country the person who committed a crime would remain an outcast for the rest of his life, whereas in the city he would be shielded by his anonymity.

Will it help to broadcast his mistakes and misfortunes and to lower him still more in the eyes of his former friends? Unless you have lived in a country community you cannot imagine the harm that can be done by destructive writing about some individual. Least of all can you imagine the heartaches, the misery and grief that parading a man's misfortunes can cause to his friends in his community. The damage that can be done to a man's family by giving publicity to his mistakes in the country paper can never be repaired. Such a story can do no good and hurts everyone in that community.[6]

A third authority, James Clifford Safley, a former publisher of a newspaper in Idaho, cautioned country editors in 1930 to "avoid publication of gossip and scandal, unless it actually becomes a matter of court record, and even then he need not indulge in it too freely, unless the case is of genuine public interest."[7]

AN EMPHASIS ON SENSATIONALISM

One of the distinguishing characteristics of yellow journalism was "scare-heads," headlines that often screamed excitement about relatively unimportant news. Early in Aull's editorship, the *Democrat*'s headlines were as sensational as those found in Hearst's *New York Journal:* "Murderer Found Naked and Mangled;" "His Feet Cut Off;" "He Was Eaten By Hogs;" "A Horrible Death;" and "The Monster Is Safe"—a story about the capture of a gila monster that had escaped from a menagerie.[8]

Some of Aull's stories were just as sensational as his headlines during this yellow journalism phase of his career. In 1904, under the headline "Caught a Tigress," he provided the following description of a woman arrested at the Frisco Depot: "Wednesday morning, there was dragged through the streets a cursing, fighting maniac that bore the semblance of a woman. Her language was so foul, that the dirtiest by-words of the street became mere polite terms of badinage in comparison." A 1912 story, "To Go to Hell vs. Don't Give a Damn," detailed a man's arrest and jury trial for allegedly telling his sister to "go to hell." The man, charged with disturbing the peace and dignity of Lamar, claimed that he merely had said, "Oh, I don't give a damn."[9]

Aull didn't have to travel far to find most of his sensational stories. Until 1909 the *Democrat* was located in the basement of the Barton County courthouse, where most of his regular news sources were officed. The elected county officials were good sources of news and gossip, and sometimes the lines blurred between the two. Such was the case with "Bride a Giantess," a 1904 story that reflects the tongue-out-of-cheek style of Aull's early *Democrat:*

> There was a scene in the Recorder's office, Monday that doesn't often occur. Just after noon a woman, who would have easily tipped the beam at four hundred strode into the office and asked for a marriage license. At her skirts followed a meek, sickly looking little man, evidently about fifty years of age. The bride to be did all of the talking as the prospective groom was so deaf that he would easily have mistaken the most terrific peal of thunder for the patter of rain drops upon a board roof. The lady said that her name was Mrs. Dora Filk, that she was blooming twenty two and that she hailed from Lockwood. Her inoffensive little victim, she gave the audience to understand, was Mr. Isaac McMain of Whitesbora [sic], Texas. The recorder issued the license, and Squire Allee [Gail Allee, the county coroner] stood quietly by, ready to pronounce the unfortunate little man's death sentence. They stood up. It looked like a Brobdinagian [sic] tying up to a Lilliputian. The little man held his hand up to his ear and craned his head toward the squire's face. He said yes to everything the squire said with a reckless desperation that could not fail to excite

admiration. The lady in a soft, subdued voice said "yessir" and the thing was over. The happy groom asked the squire "how much?" and the latter yelled "two dollars!" But the little fellow didn't understand. The recorder took a long, deep inspiration; got his mouth down to the little fellow's ear and yelled "two dollars," so loud that the clock swayed back and forth unsteadily upon the shelf. The little man got out his wallet and fished out two iron dollars. The bride was feeling mighty good. The little groom reached out and began to fondle one of her ponderous hands in one of his. She tittered. Then she said, "Law! that's cheap. First time I got married, it cost five dollars." The recorder told her that the county had been ruined by the last two republican administrations and that prices were going to pieces. Then she volunteered the information that "he" came very near not getting her. The statement had a depressing effect upon every body present. It reminded them all how near a man would come to escaping destruction only to be gathered in at last. After this, hand in hand, they went out, making a straight line for a picture gallery to throw away some more of the little man's good money, in committing the travesty to a pasteboard card.[10]

NEWS SOURCES

Aull made a habit of dropping by the county offices in the courthouse twice a day. Other daily stops included city hall, the schools, the churches, the jails, the hospitals, the funeral homes, and businesses around the square. Short of copy one July day in 1902, he conducted a formal interview with the local undertaker, Hoyt Humphrey, believing that his "gruesome experiences in taking care of the dead" might interest readers of the *Democrat*. Humphrey didn't disappoint. The mortician/furniture store owner gave Aull a guided tour of his operation and enthralled him with tales of the macabre. Among the things Humphrey displayed in an upstairs room, Aull recounted for his readers, were the "good right arm" of a murderer lynched in Barton County ten years earlier and the embalmed foot of a well-known local man.[11]

Aull's best news source throughout most of his career was the barber shop, where he began each day with an 8 A.M. shave. Until the electric razor came along in the 1930s, men gathered in Lamar's barber shops every morning to discuss such topics as politics, crop conditions, and how the fish were biting in Muddy Creek. Four or five "tonsorial parlors" operated in Lamar, but Aull preferred Will Jones's four-chair shop on the northwest corner of the square for the latest gossip. Jones was a colorful character who liked to boast that he had shaved President McKinley and John D. Rockefeller. He inadvertently supplied Aull with a juicy story early one November morning in 1917 when he scuffled with a fellow barber in his shop. Much to the editor's disappointment, however, the fisticuffs occurred thirty minutes before his arrival and he was unable to provide an eyewitness account. Still, Aull managed to turn up all the details, and that afternoon's *Democrat* carried a blow-by-blow account of the barbers' fight.[12]

After spending most of the morning making his rounds and gathering the stories for his 3:30 P.M. edition, Aull usually returned to the *Democrat* office around noon and began writing. "He didn't stop for lunch," recalled his youngest daughter, Betty Aull White, who worked for the *Democrat* after graduating from the University of Missouri School of Journalism in 1930. "He found that this was his best time to write. People kind of left him alone then."[13]

Everything was written in longhand, for Aull never learned—or cared—to use a typewriter or any of the other equipment in the *Democrat* office. "If I were a printer or a [L]inotype operator I wouldn't have the time to get out and get the news and give the people the kind of a newspaper they want," he told a *Kansas City Star* reporter in 1937. Consequently, he churned out stories, editorials, and other bits of wisdom and gossip as fast as he could to fill the pages of an afternoon daily. At times, he felt overwhelmed by his paper's insatiable demand for copy: "The typos [typesetters] eat and grind the stuff as fast as he can hang it on the hook, and keep yelling for more. He is hounded and bully-ragged for copy until it becomes a nightmare, but still he must grind away, for the paper must be gotten out. Then, when he has dug around for twenty-four hours, trying to find something that will interest his readers, it makes him feel truly ecstatic to have them intimate to him that his paper 'ain't no count.' "[14]

Some news items simply walked in the door, courtesy of advertisers, farmers in town on business, or rural letter carriers who picked up tidbits of information on their routes. Though Aull appreciated these "personals" for their value as space fillers, the constant interruptions disrupted his routine. A 1921 ad in the *Democrat* encouraged readers to telephone Elsie Brown in the office with their local news from ten o'clock to noon every morning. Aull also took to hiding at his desk be-hind the Linotype machine to avoid the steady stream of visitors.[15]

A SHORTAGE OF COPY

The *Democrat*'s reputation as a scandal sheet came about because of Aull's zeal to provide his readers with the latest "red-hot news," but also for the simple reason that he didn't have the luxury of turning many stories away. A one-man reporting staff for most of his career, he fre-quently scrambled to scrape up enough copy to fill a six-day daily. He disdained the "boiler plate" material that other country newspapers used in sometimes endless quantities to supplement their news coverage. Fur-ther compounding Aull's problem was the fact that at least two other Lamar newspapers competed against him during the entire time he owned the *Democrat*. If the *Leader* or the *Republican* broke a good story first, Aull looked elsewhere for something his readers would enjoy. He did publish items from other papers in Barton County and southwest Missouri on occasion, but seldom anything from his rivals in town.

As far as newspaper towns went, Lamar offered little out of the ordi-nary except its status as the county seat and a magnificent public square around which most of the town's businesses were located. Yet for twenty-six of the forty-eight years Aull published the *Democrat,* he had to contend with another daily paper in Lamar. With a population rang-ing from 2,255 to 2,992 during Aull's editorship, Lamar was one of the smallest towns in the United States to boast two dailies during this time.[16]

Aull scoured the town for anything that would give him a leg up on the competition and allow him to fill the four or six pages of the *Daily Democrat*. Pad and pencil always in hand, he was a familiar sight around the courthouse square as he made his way to each office, bank, and store. According to an unpublished manuscript by Frank Popplewell, a Missouri historian who lived in Lamar in the 1920s, Aull always wore a big coat with its tails floating "in the breeze stirred by his rapid stride from place to place" and its pockets bulging with "copious notes."[17]

Despite his meticulous news coverage, a town the size of Lamar sim-ply had days in which nothing happened. Two years after converting the *Democrat* to daily publication, Aull expressed his frustration: "As we have told our readers before there are days, when there's no danger, of a fellow getting out a 'yellow' daily in a country town. Thursday was such a day in Lamar. Nobody died, nobody got married, nobody got into a fight, and if there were any social functions on tap, we were not put next. This is the kind of a day that makes a country newspaper man want to throw up his job." The former schoolteacher questioned his career choice aloud now and then: "Sometimes, we sit here and wonder why any fool wants to undertake to get out more than a monthly paper, in the average county seat town. We always have this spell of wondering, when one of these streaks of dull, do nothing days come upon us, with no fights, lawsuits, divorces nor even a crap game. It's truly an awful time, though they do say happy is the little old town that has no history."[18]

With news of a sensational nature often in short supply in Lamar, requests to keep certain items out of the *Democrat* always fell on deaf ears. Two frequent remarks particularly irked Aull: "I wouldn't put this in the paper," and "Now that damned fool will put what you said in the paper, if you don't look out."[19] Such comments served only to remind Aull that his subscribers would be eager to read what someone else was so anxious to have withheld. In 1918 he admonished those who made such demands in presenting his philosophy of country journalism:

> Perhaps it never occurred to you that even after we've swept the whole gossip and happenings of a village of twenty-five hundred souls, we are still short of enough stuff to get out the little old paper that must be gotten off, somehow, six times a week. The big papers have the world for a field. The little ones [*sic*] has only its own tiny corner, from which to glean. But fortunately the doings and sayings of its limited field, faithfully set forth, are of more interest to the average man or woman than what's happening in the royal court at London. Otherwise, the small sheet would not exist. But since it is so restricted in its field, the local sheet must grind all that comes to the mill. If it turns any grist away its pages are either empty, or else filled up with a lot of stale stuff from the outside that has been read and re-read in the larger papers.[20]

When the news flowed freely, it was easy to put out a daily newspaper in a country town. But the most exciting news Aull could dig up some days was that "Mrs. Somebody goes out to the country to visit some rural cousins." On these all-too-frequent occasions, as the *Democrat*'s copy boy hollered for more and more items to fill the paper, Aull considered him the "devil" incarnate. "At least, you'd about as soon see the real devil coming as you would your office devil," he confided to readers.[21]

To help ease the copy shortage, in 1910 the editor started sprinkling several fictitious characters on his commentary pages. Aull's readers knew these characters were made up, and at no time did anyone ever mistake their antics for legitimate news coverage. The Rev. Hardscrabble was ancient and dignified, John Henry Meeks was lowly and humble but industrious, Bill and Mandy Spivins always quarreled, Samantha Scroggs was a sour and sharp-tongued old maid, Mary Ellen Sparks was a gossip, and Selma Sniff was angry much of the time. Readers sometimes tried to determine if these characters represented actual people in Lamar, but it is unlikely they did. Through them, Aull was able to reveal quirks of human nature and find an outlet for his creative writing. The Presbyterian ladies, at a tea one June afternoon in 1922, even staged the "wedding" of Kewpie Kewps and Mable Mott. Most of Aull's characters were impersonated by the women. The Rev. Hardscrabble performed the ceremony, the best man was Ebenezer Wise, and the bridesmaid was Sophronia Patch. John Henry Meeks gave the bride away, Mandy Spivins sang "I Love You Truly," and Samantha Scroggs played the piano. The flower girls were Selma Sniff and Ima Kritik.[22]

Unlike Ed Howe and William Allen White, Aull could not escape the daily grind of publishing a newspaper by traveling throughout the United States or abroad. When he did leave Lamar, it was for only a day or two to attend a meeting of the Missouri Press Association. And even then, he had to prepare enough copy in advance to cover his absence. Much to his chagrin, though, sometimes his readers didn't even notice that he had been away. A one-day trip in 1904 prompted the following comment: "The editor of the *Democrat* was out of town, Monday, and before he left, he wrote what he thought were some passable editorial paragraphs. When he came home and looked at the paper and saw what the printers had done to him, in setting the said paragraphs up, he became fully reconciled to a fact that he had always, before, sincerely regretted, viz, that nobody reads the editorials."[23]

Mistakes by the *Democrat*'s print shop in typesetting Aull's copy were a constant source of irritation to the editor. He had little time to proof the galleys before they went to press, and many of the minor revisions he requested were misplaced in the confusion. Aware of the frenetic pace his printers maintained, such typographical errors as "a woman's carrier" instead of "a woman's career" still caused Aull to "tear his hair, and beat his breast."[24]

He occasionally came across situations where it was a formidable task just to ascertain a news subject's name. While most country editors would settle for "Mr. Smith" or "Mr. Jones" in identifying a newcomer or a stranger to town who had run into some trouble, Aull insisted on tracking down the person's full name. "You might have to walk several blocks and see three or four different persons, after you had every part of your story complete, except one man's prefix letters," he explained in 1929. Aull wouldn't accept nicknames, either. Initials were fine, but he refused to refer to someone as "Tater Blank" when it was obvious that "Tater" wasn't the man's given name.[25]

TELLING IT LIKE IT IS

Anyone in Barton County who did anything out of the ordinary could find an account of his or her transgression in the *Democrat*. Aull considered Ed Howe the "best human interest reporter in the world" and took note of the juicy scandals appearing in his *Atchison* (Kans.) *Globe*. He took Howe's premise that "the wages of sin is publicity" to heart, and that became the standard by which he judged the newsworthiness of any story.[26]

For those in Lamar or Barton County who may have wondered why he broke all the traditional rules of journalism in making private facts public, Aull periodically provided a justification. In 1917 he claimed that "publishing the facts about an embarrassing matter is a good deal like opening a boil. The whole thing is emptied out, and the sore heals. By publishing the facts, we don't mean persistently lying about them or misrepresenting them. We mean actually giving them as nearly as possible like they are."[27] Four years later, he defended the scandalous character of the *Democrat:*

> All of us gossip, the last one of us, and most of it is inspired by a sort of cross between malice and curiosity. Yet, whenever we hear a man or a woman break out on a tirade against gossips and gossipers, it makes us suspicious. Some way, we feel like their objections are personal. Gossip gets at the very root of human nature. It's like a hedge.

It's full of thorns, but it makes it hard to get off the high and proper road. We would say that it would be fine if we could send the worst gossipers to hell, and at the same time, be careful that their ill-natured and interesting remarks, about ourselves, didn't contain too much truth.[28]

Arthur Aull was despised by many in Lamar, but most read his *Democrat*. If they refused to subscribe, they managed to borrow someone else's copy. "Nearly everyone in the vicinity of Lamar in the 1930s either cussed or discussed Aull," said Richard Jones, publisher of the *Sheldon* (Mo.) *Enterprise* in the 1940s. "His ability to 'tell it like it is' was spreading from coast to coast. People were subscribing to the *Democrat* who had never heard of Lamar except for Arthur Aull." In a 1972 interview, Lamar resident Pat Earp recalled that her grandmother tried to hide the *Democrat* before she could read it but wasn't always successful.[29]

A review of the *Democrat*'s sometimes scurrilous content would lead one to comprehend more fully the nation's fascination with the paper and the grandmother's concern. Nothing titillated readers of the *Democrat* more than Aull's coverage of divorce day in Barton County Circuit Court. He liked to point out that Friday traditionally was "hangman's day" throughout the civilized world, but in Lamar it was "the day of Cupid's local death knell." With as many as fifteen divorce cases on the docket some days, Aull had ample opportunity to find something scandalous that would appeal to his readers. He diligently examined the divorce petitions and listened to the testimony before the judge for anything of a salacious nature. He justified his approach in 1902: "Nearly all of the readers of newspapers are 'strictly moral' yet there is nothing [that] so arouses their interest as an article that tells about one man running off with another man's wife."[30]

One such incident was reported in the *Democrat* in 1927 and reprinted in *Life* and other magazines years later. Aull's original story read, in part: "Jim Ray Sloan, of Oskaloosa, was divorced from his wife, Mary Ellen. Mrs. Sloan ran off with her brother-in-law while her husband and the children were at the Baptist church, having gone out from the services to join him, leaving her husband inside with their three children." The snippet in *Life* eighteen years later was altered slightly, apparently to avoid an invasion of privacy or libel suit: "John Jones was divorced from his wife, Ella, at the courthouse Tuesday. Mrs. Jones ran off with her brother-in-law while her husband and children were at the Baptist Church."[31]

Other divorce stories revealed considerably more and were much too vulgar for a popular magazine to reprint, even with modifications. But in the *Democrat* such items were expected, and readers would have been disappointed had Aull omitted any of the scurrilous details. Some stories even revealed the names of men with whom wives had committed adultery. Under such headlines as "She Wanted a Divorce, and She Wanted It Bad," "The Tragedies That Follow the Altar," and "They Tell Their Marital Woes," Aull's divorce stories contained many shocking statements of an extremely personal nature. He disclosed every prurient detail even though the newsworthiness of such items was minimal.

The following accounts are representative of Aull's style, always told from the petitioner's point of view:

> Frank Kester, a man in his early forties, was divorced from his wife, Verna Marie Kester. They were married, in Colorado, August 25th, 1915, and lived together about eighteen months. She had an awful temper, he said, and would fly into a rage, upon the most trivial occasion. She told him she didn't love him. She wouldn't cook his meals, nor keep the house in order. She took night rides with other men, and permitted them to take improper liberties with her. When he protested, she told him, she would do as she pleased, and for him to go to hell. . . .[32]

> Robert C. Millard was divorced from his wife Anna. The latter, apparently, could never content herself with just one man. Not long after they were married, they went to Webb City to live. Anna got pretty familiar with a man, that came around, every day, to take orders for a local grocery. He got in the habit of staying in the house with Anna, a whole lot longer, than it would take, even a very slow man, to get up an order for groceries. . . .[33]

> James Parks, nineteen years old, was divorced from his wife, Charlotte Esther. They were married the ninth of last June and came to Lamar, to live at the home of Jim's father, Frank Parks. Jim worked nights, at one of the garages. He would get home, late in the morning, or forenoon, sometimes it would be ten o'clock. There would be no breakfast, and she would usually be in bed. His father would be out, walking around the yard, waiting for his breakfast. She wouldn't cook,

and she told Jim flatly she didn't care for him. He did not satisfy her marital cravings. She ran around with other men, notably the young Cane Hill blacksmith, who was later arrested for issuing fraudulent checks. . . .[34]

Anna Anglen brings a suit for divorce, in which her charges are morbid and unusual . . . Then, she says, because of an abnormal sex development of the defendant, their relations as husband and wife could not be maintained without great pain and physical anguish to her. The doctors advised her, when she was compelled to seek their aid, that they could do nothing for her, until marital relations ceased. Her husband, she said, showed her no consideration. He insisted upon his connubial rights as remorselessly as Shylock did for the pound of flesh, finally telling her the only way out of it was for her to go get a divorce. . . .[35]

Mr. and Mrs. Finney were married in the state of Wyoming, April 1st, 1922. They lived together until about December first, save for some previous separations, which were his fault. She charges that he often cursed and abused her, called her a bitch and other foul names, and since last Christmas has deserted her and failed to provide for her. . . . She says she has seen the defendant commit sodomy on the person of a cow, and he has forced her to submit to the marital act in the presence of the children. . . .[36]

Aull enjoyed describing a comical divorce proceeding as much as he did a scandalous one. When a man divorced his wife after forty-three years of marriage, Aull quipped: "Mr. Kelsey says he'd have stayed with it to the end, seeing that he stuck so well, but it was just simply 'Hell.' " On another occasion, a seventy-two-year-old woman left her seventy-nine-year-old husband after only five months of marriage. "They'd been sleeping without sheets and slips and she told him she was going to buy some," Aull reported. "He was against it. He'd slept without sheets and pillow cases for years and it was good enough. No use wasting good money on them."[37]

Aull sometimes spent as much time studying the women involved in Barton County divorce proceedings as he did their petitions. It is evident he felt a good deal of physical attraction toward some of the women:

She wore a big, dark hat, which formed a fine background for her really pretty face. She was tastily dressed in black, with a skirt, built along modern lines to show off the salient points of her plump, round figure.[38]

Mrs. Heigle has blue eyes and the most wonderful blond hair in Lamar. She has a voluptous [sic] figure and is a young woman of stunning appearance.[39]

Pauline is a girl that one would think a young man would work his fingernails off to support, rather than try to live off her. She is tall, not at all fat, but with a figure that suggests voluptuousness.[40]

Mrs. Campbell is an unusually good looking woman. She has light brown hair, regular handsome features, a full but shapely figure, and much of what the movie fans, three or four years ago would have called 'It' or feminine appeal.[41]

Aull's descriptions weren't always flattering, however:

Mrs. Hendricks is a rather short, stout motherly looking old lady. . . .[42]

She frankly looks like she wasn't very sweet tempered.[43]

Mrs. Greenwood is a tall, spare woman, with light hair, who looks as if she had seen a hard time. She must be about forty.[44]

In the course of witnessing thousands of divorce proceedings, Aull naturally developed some strong beliefs about marriage. Some were unusual, others were typical of his era. Divorced men and women were almost becoming the rule rather than the exception, he declared, noting that the divorce rate in Kansas City and other urban areas was approaching 50 percent. He attributed the rising divorce rate to several factors: the unwillingness of some men to earn a decent living and support their wives; clashing personalities and tastes; sexual incompatibility; and "diseased dispositions," which included "nagging, whining, suspicion and self-pity on the part of women, drunkenness or disposition towards tyranny on the part of men." With nine out of ten divorce petitions being filed by women, Aull believed still another cause was their desire to gain freedom and independence.[45]

Bucking the conventional wisdom of the day, Aull maintained that it wasn't necessary for a marriage to last until one of the partners died. He questioned, "If a marriage has gone on the rocks, why not acknowledge it?" It was his experience that, despite what everyone thought, few couples considered divorce until they had exhausted every opportunity for reconciliation and approached the point of desperation. "Divorce may be carried too far," he wrote in 1935, "but how often it is a legal and a decent escape from conditions that are intolerable—conditions that make the very term of wedlock a sardonic and leering mockery!"[46]

Aull contended that marriage was "purely a woman's game" and alimony should be abolished, except when children were involved. Hardened by the number of divorces he had observed firsthand in Barton County, he believed the very institution of marriage was rapidly disappearing. Men and women would still form unions for "proper sexual relations," he wrote, and these partnerships could be maintained with their own set of laws and procedures.[47]

Aull freely offered his views on birth control at a time when most editors were reluctant even to broach the subject. On one hand, he felt that the development of contraception gave rise to "unconventional sex relations with little danger of pregnancy." Women who were disposed to the "philandering practices" might be encouraged to freely participate knowing they were protected from the "natural results of their transgressions." But the advantages clearly outweighed any undesired effects. Aull believed that few women really desired more than two or three children and would welcome a contraceptive device that allowed them to dictate the size of their families. "The average woman who bears and rears a large family, goes through much more than does a soldier on a score of bloody fields," he said in support of birth control in 1936.[48] Furthermore, he believed birth control was necessary to prevent an economic calamity by 1995—half the population would be at least sixty years old.

Along with the divorce accounts came tales of seduction, alienation of affection, bestiality, and other forms of immoral conduct. Unlike his first few years on the *Democrat* when he repeatedly scrambled to find something sensational, he subsequently discovered that the county courthouse supplied enough scandal to satisfy all the town gossips. The editor checked any complaint filed or warrant issued and attended every preliminary hearing and jury trial of the circuit court. Aull's trial coverage became one of his specialties, and although it never received the widespread publicity as did his scintillating anecdotes, it was actually much more shocking.

MORALLY OFFENSIVE MEDIUM

Aull considered a 1940 sodomy trial in Barton County Circuit Court "the most unusual and sensational" court proceeding perhaps in the history of the entire southwest portion of the state.[49] When a traveling piano salesman was charged with attempting to rape a nineteen-year-old Nevada, Missouri, woman, in his Dodge pickup truck, Aull immediately sensed the story was more sensational than even the preliminary information indicated. The case had all the requisite elements: an attractive, well-known victim; a sinister-looking defendant; the use of alcohol; adultery; and, of course, plenty of prurient details.

As the trial unfolded, Aull informed his readers, among other things, that the young woman was a virgin and the defendant was "a powerful young pervert" who had "thrust his tongue into the vulva." Much of the testimony centered on whether the woman had been drinking and a willing participant, and how the salesman could have committed sodomy without removing her panties. The Barton County prosecuting attorney attempted to discount the defense's latter argument: "Gentlemen, it's not material whether they were pulled off or not. All you gentlemen have certainly in your own experience or observation known about a woman's panties!" Aull's story ended with the following remark: "He let it rest there—which was both wise and discreet."[50]

In the end, the salesman was acquitted on the sodomy charge because, as one juror told Aull, "When I thought of my daughter, I felt I ought to convict him. When I thought of my boy I figured maybe I ought to turn him loose." The defendant was tried again, this time for the attempted rape, and convicted. But the jury fined him only fifty dollars and court costs because of the extenuating circumstances. Aull, at first compassionate toward the victim, took more of a detached stance editorially after hearing talk around town that she was a "fast girl" and that her conduct may have invited such an attack. Rather, he shifted his sympathies to the defendant's wife, whom he described as "the epitome of woe, sadness and distress" as she sat by her husband's side throughout the trial.[51]

Victims of rape and incest were always named by the *Democrat,* even when minors were involved. One of the last stories Aull wrote before a kidney disorder forced his retirement from the paper involved the arrest of a man for the attempted rape of a three-year-old girl behind a stack of tiles. The child and her assailant were identified according to the *Demo-*

crat's policy even though her parents initially preferred not to press charges since the man had not accomplished his purpose. Aull himself was a witness in a 1942 case in which a seventy-year-old man was convicted of statutory assault on a ten-year-old girl who helped care for the man's invalid wife. Aull testified for the prosecution that he overheard the man say he had held the girl on his lap and fondled her.[52]

Juveniles charged with criminal offenses were also named by the *Democrat*. This, too, set Aull apart from nearly all his contemporaries. According to Charles Laurel Allen, assistant dean and director of research at the Medill School of Journalism at Northwestern University, most country newspapers of the late 1920s presented only the vaguest facts of juvenile delinquency and omitted the names or any statements that would identify the perpetrators. This was to avoid making the child an outcast from his peers and bringing disgrace to his parents.[53] Aull, however, made no distinction between a juvenile and adult offender and faithfully followed his tell-everything rule.

When little Orville Ray Coates confessed to breaking into mailboxes at the post office, taking several letters and checks, and hiding them under the corner of his house, the *Democrat*'s headline, "An Eight Year Old Mail Robber," helped draw attention to the lengthy story. When ten-year-old Albert Regan broke into the Lamar Steam Laundry and robbed the money drawer, that story made the front page of the paper. When fifteen-year-old Claude Mann was arrested for breaking into the home of a family away at Sunday school and stealing a couple of pocketknives, Aull reported that "he seems either to be a kleptomaniac or a moral degenerate." And when thirteen-year-old Geraldine Walker showed up "dead drunk" at the courthouse one Saturday afternoon, Aull dutifully described all the conditions of the boy's vomiting.[54]

Aull reported any suicide or attempted suicide in a matter-of-fact manner with little accompanying editorial comment. Still, his step-by-step depictions of how the suicides were committed violated all the traditional rules of newspapering. Those in Lamar or Barton County who contemplated killing themselves had only to read the *Democrat* for a virtual instruction manual. For example:

> She had taken two flour sacks, that were torn down the side into dish cloths, and tied the corners at each end together, making a loop, not unlike a horse collar. One end was looped over the end of the door, and the other she placed under her chin. It is the general belief

that she stood upon the trunk as she placed the noose under her chin and jumped off. This belief is strengthened by the fact that there is a bruised place at the side of the forehead, as if her head had violently struck the door. Death came from strangulation and not from the un-jointing of the vertebrae. She held up her feet while she was choking, and after the end they sank back to the floor.[55]

After hearing of a suicide, Aull usually visited the site as quickly as possible. He would record a graphic description of the scene, then quiz friends and relatives of the victim to determine a motive. If the individual suffered from an incurable disease or mental illness, Aull tended to believe the suicide was justified, and his stories reflected his empathy. But when he could make no sense of the deceased's actions, his tone was unpitying. In 1939, when a man killed himself after complaining that his wife's coffee was too hot, Aull made no effort to hide his disgust. The *Democrat*'s headline read, "Splattered Brains and Blood All Over His Three Children."[56]

Aull's constant quest for the grim and grisly turned even his own stomach at times. Death fascinated him, and when Barton County Sheriff Bill Noble invited him in 1923 to witness the hanging of two men convicted of murdering a Carthage, Missouri, grocer, he readily accepted even though it meant leaving Lamar at 3 A.M. But after arriving at the Carthage jail where a crowd of at least two thousand awaited the daybreak executions in a "holiday like" mood, Aull soon realized the horror of what was to come. He later wrote a first-person account of the experience: "How I wished I could have recalled my decision to come, and remain away from the sickening business! True enough, I could have shouldered my way out. I thought of this but there was an uneasy fascination in staying to see the blacks die, besides the humiliation of going to witness a hanging and then not having the stomach to stay and see it through."[57] Of course, leaving the scene prematurely meant missing the story, and so Aull stayed. As repulsed as he was, he managed to note every writhing, twisting, and squirming movement of the two men as they met their death.

The fact that two thousand men, women, and children turned out at 5 A.M. to view an execution reinforced Aull's belief that the stories which drew the greatest response "are those which tell of agony and misfortune."[58] Throughout his career he strove to provide his readers with what they wanted even though some of the ghastly sights he recorded made him nauseated. He was called to an inquest at the River Funeral Home one Sunday in 1943 to view the aftermath of the "most horrible accident in the history of Barton County." A woman was thrown under the edge of an overturning transport truck carrying twenty thousand pounds of mining machinery and decapitated. Aull forced himself to look at what remained of the body to provide a full description in Monday's *Democrat*. Of the thousands of stories he wrote for the paper, his account of her death would surpass all for grisly detail:

> One moment Mrs. Rosy Chikowsky sat in the car beside her husband, talking, observing, as these two with their daughter, Nellie Doucey, were making their way from Ft. Scott to West Plains, a second or two later what was once this lively, intelligent woman of sixty three, was a shapeless mass of mashed and ground muscles and bones, soaked with blood, and insensible. The head was severed from the body, the bones of the skull were mashed to pieces, the brains gone, only the hair and the skin, which covered the head, two seconds before, were to be found. In the orifice left at the top of the chest, when the neck was severed, the heart, still quivering, the lungs and parts of the smaller intestine were thrust up through the top of the human trunk. The legs were mashed and broken, until they had no form. It was the most gruesome and appalling remnant of human flesh that was ever conveyed in a Barton County hearse to the room of death.[59]

Aull's daily visits to the two physician-operated hospitals in Lamar produced a good deal of material that wasn't newsworthy by conventional standards. Readers of the *Democrat* often knew more about a patient's condition than the patient herself. Some of the details, though, were provided more out of curiosity's sake than necessity. Readers hardly needed to know that a tumor weighing five and a half pounds and as big as a half-gallon bucket was removed from Mae Hylton's abdomen. Or that 192 gallstones, almost enough to fill a two-ounce bottle, were removed from Mrs. Ted Wealand's cyst. Even Luanna Aull couldn't escape her husband's incessant glare. Her "terible [*sic*] nausea" woke him at 5 A.M., he reported one day, adding that she was "the sickest woman we ever saw."[60]

After word of Aull's sensational brand of journalism began filtering out in the late 1930s and 1940s, he inevitably was asked to expound on his print-everything philosophy. He had told readers of the *Democrat* before that running a newspaper was a good deal like running a grocery

store—the proprietor had to search constantly for something that customers would plunk money down for. Aull's wares were the "little
chunks of town gossip." But when the large newspapers and national
magazines came inquiring, his explanation took a more noble slant. By
making all scandalous conduct public knowledge, he maintained, he
was effectually eliminating all need for gossip. He gave nearly the same
word-for-word rationale to the *Chicago Daily News* in 1943 and the *St.
Louis Post-Dispatch* in 1946: "It's always been my theory that if you air a
thing in print, even a big scandal, you'll do the folks concerned more
good than if you try to ignore it. When I get through with an unsavory
story there is nothing left for the people to gossip about."[61]

But as far as Jennie Wirts and Don O'Neal were concerned, Aull had
given readers of the *Democrat* more than enough to gossip about. Their
story was the talk of the town for weeks, and even today a large number
of townspeople are familiar with the circumstances surrounding their
1939 marriage. *Life* called it the most sensational story ever to appear in
the *Democrat* and reprinted much of it six years later.[62] The story also
made the *Journal of the American Medical Association.* Yet Aull's original
article ran with little fanfare in the *Democrat,* devoid of a headline, and
at the bottom of page two:

> At 7:30 p.m. Monday an eight and a half pound son was born to
> Miss Jennie Wirts, book keeper for the Lamar Trust. At nine o'clock
> Don O'Neal, cashier of the bank, stood by her bed, and they were
> married by Rev. Martin Pope. Miss Jennie had been at her work in the
> bank, every day, until Monday, when she was detained by some symp-
> toms, she did not understand. No one in the bank who daily worked
> side by side with her, suspected that she was in a condition of expec-
> tant motherhood. This included the cashier Don O'Neal, the father of
> her child. She remained at home, Monday, and along in the afternoon
> Dr. Bickel was called. She told him she was suffering from severe
> cramps. Dr. Bickel made a brief examination and told her she seemed
> to be at the end of pregnancy. She was sure this could not be. He
> asked her if her periods of menstruation had not ceased a good many
> months ago. She said, Yes, they came no more after last September
> until in March there was some evidence of a recurrence, but not nor-
> mal. However, she was not impressed by this absence of natural phe-
> nomenon. The physician asked if she had not felt "motion." She was
> plainly at a loss until he explained this almost universal evidence of de-
> veloping life in a woman's womb. Apparently by the time the physi-

cian was called the head of the child had descended into the pelvis, as childbirth was approaching, so this left the physician momentarily at something of a loss as to the mass in the abdomen. But as the symptoms progressed he saw it was an undeniable case of labor. After this, word was sent to Mr. O'Neal. Then, somewhat later when Dr. Bickel had assured the patient that there could be no mistaking the case, she had him call Mr. O'Neal. Later the doctor had a talk with Don. The latter said he and Jennie had long intended to get married. But she kept up the home for her brother, Robert, and his children were not yet settled in life, so they had put it off from time to time, neither of them realizing her condition. He said, of course, the baby could be spirited away, placed in an institution and there would be no public knowledge of its existence. But he'd go down before the evening was over and marry Jennie, they would keep and rear the baby, tell the whole truth about it, and make no effort to sidestep or conceal and certainly not to disinherit it, by rushing it into orphaned anononimity [*sic*]. The baby was born at 7:30. It was a fine eight and a half pound boy. Don got a marriage license, and, as Jennie's pastor, Rev. De-Lozier, was out of town, he obtained the services of Rev. Martin T. Pope. At nine o'clock he stood by Jennie's bedside while the minister conducted the brief service that made them man and wife. The bride is thirty-three, the groom, fifty-three. None of the folks at the bank where Miss Jennie worked day after day, suspected. There wasn't apparently a whisper from sharp eyed gossips. Mr. O'Neal was plainly taken by complete surprise, but he never wavered in his decision to make no attempt at concealment [*sic*] or evasion. The very remarkable situation, no one can deny, brought forth in a really dramatic manner his manly courage and sense of deep regard for a sacred responsibility. In the mean time, for a few days, there will be a great ohing! and ahing! in and about the town. But soon, since no concealment has been made of the facts, it will no longer stir gossipy interest. Don and Jennie, fine couple as they are, will stand forth with their little son, secure as ever in the public esteem and their united lives will move on peacefully, usefully and in honor. We could have said we were married secretly say a year or two ago, Don told a friend. But it wasn't that way and we're not going to lie.[63]

Aull then abandoned the story for good, except to add a brief editorial comment: "Well, true enough, there never was a better girl than Jennie, and we all know Don is a grand old boy, but God! it was badly managed." He reminded readers that shortly before the 1884 presiden-

tial election Grover Cleveland refused to deny charges that he had fa-
thered an unmarried woman's child some years before. Cleveland instructed his campaign staff to "tell the truth," and he was elected.[64]

COMMUNITY RESPONSE

Aull realized early on that aside from a juicy scandal, subscribers to
the *Democrat* enjoyed the editor "catching hell" more than anything
else. He once related the story of a veteran newspaperman giving a new
editor some advice. The former, noticing that the latter had been publishing quite a few complimentary items about himself, reminded his
younger colleague: "[T]he only thing about you the readers of the paper
get a real kick out of, is where you get a nice hard knock. If you see any
good low down knocks on yourself, of course, you don't have to print
'em in your own paper. But remember your readers would sure enjoy
'em."[65] Whether Aull was the young editor is not known, but he did
follow the bit of wisdom faithfully. All letters to the editor were published, as long as they contained a valid signature. As scathing as some
were, the letters helped Aull fill the *Democrat* on slow news days, and
they were among the best-read pieces in the paper. These three are in-
dicative of the kind he received:

> Mr. Lamar Democrat—you will Please stop that Paper as I Never
> subscribed for the Paper and I don't want it at any Price. [I]t makes
> me mad to read it and I Prefer to not have it on my place now. Please
> Stop it at once.[66]

> I have been a reader of the Lamar Democrat for just a few months,
> but I am thoroly [*sic*] disgusted with the unclean thoughts that are
> clearly expressed.
> In the many years that I have been a reader of large city newspa-
> pers, it is seldom that I ever read an evil minded editorial.
> Rotten gossip is spread freely enough, without printing it in the
> daily papers. Therefore helping to corrupt what good morals young-
> sters, from 10 years up, may possess. . . .[67]

> If you can spare me the space in your filthy sheet, I would like to
> answer some of the D— lies in Feb. 22 eddits in which you should be

like the great and noted president Washington and not tell so many
D— lies. As stated my wife did not know where I had gone and taken
the baby. Who is four and [a] half years old instead of 20 months old
as your lie stated. . . .[68]

A majority of the letters addressed problems with accuracy. Aull
based many stories on hearsay and rushed them into print before cor-
roborating all the facts. Some of his mistakes were particularly embarrassing, such as his announcement that Clara Belle Davidson had
married Carl Wood on May 16, 1919, in Carthage, Missouri. Davidson
at the time lived in Wyoming, Wood in Iowa. Both insisted on a rebut-
tal. "I don't doubt your having heard it," Davidson wrote, "but it does
seem you specialize on publishing false weddings."[69]
One reader, accused by Aull of participating in a duck killing at a
farmer's pond, stated that the editor's "usual formula—One third gossip, and two thirds imagination" caused the inaccuracy. Aull seldom defended the veracity of a story after receiving a complaint. Rather, he
seized the opportunity to air his mistake publicly. Under the headline
"We Pulled a Good One," for example, he explained that he had greatly
erred in reporting a wealthy steam shovel owner's arrest in connection
with a post office robbery. "You know, occasionally, by misunderstand-
ing what somebody says, as we go about, gathering up the daily dope,
we'll pull a bone just about the same size and of similar contour and ori-
gin to the one with which Samson slew the Philistines," he admitted.[70]
Aull's most vocal critic was the Rev. Ralph Ward of the local
Methodist-Episcopalian church. Ward invited Aull to his church one
Sunday night in May 1936 under the pretext that his sermon would
focus on newspapers. Much to Aull's surprise, the minister took the occasion to denounce him before the congregation. Ward read a selection
from one of Aull's "Pore Weak Human Nature" columns containing
the exclamations Jesus!, God!, and Hell!, claiming that such expressions
were "equal to profaning a man's mother." He went on to say that Aull
too frequently used the language of the street and that his newspaper
wasn't suitable for a family to read. He told the congregation that many
in town needed a revival, but no one more than the man who ran the
Democrat.[71]
Aull took the affront good-naturedly, headlining his story "Rev.
Ward Takes Yours Truly to the Woodshed" and stating that he would

seriously consider the preacher's offer to occupy the pulpit and respond to the charges. The *Kansas City Times* recognized the hilarity of the situation and reprinted Aull's story in its entirety on the front page.[72]

The editor never did accept Ward's invitation to return to the church. Ward continued to snipe at Aull, objecting to every off-color word in the *Democrat*. When Aull used the phrase "damned fool" in one of his "Pepper and Salt" columns, the minister responded in a letter to the editor: "That last expression is not nice and many of us wish you would not use it, and others of a similar sort, in our home paper." But before Ward left Lamar in 1939, the two had developed a mutual admiration. Aull felt that he had finally met someone in Lamar whose knowledge of world affairs rivaled his own. Ward would drop by the *Democrat* office on occasion and engage Aull in a debate over pacifism or isolationism.[73]

Several irate readers didn't bother writing a letter to the editor or rebuking Aull in public; they barged into the *Democrat* office or knocked on the door of his home. He laughed off the easily controllable threats under such headlines as "Mrs. Jackson Gets Into Our Wool" and "Don't Shoot the Fiddler, He's Doing His Best." In the latter case, a woman dropped by the newspaper one afternoon in 1938 and told Aull, "I nearly got killed today, and if you have anything in about it and it's twisted around and wrong, I'm going to come in and make you eat the paper, word by word." Sometimes the complaints were more laughable than endangering, as in this 1920 anecdote from the *Democrat:* "A man came in the other day, and told us he was getting mighty damned sick of the things we put in the paper. We asked him what he would suggest as a change. He said, well, for one thing, he'd like to see an item in there, occasionally, about himself."[74]

Others insisted that their names or other details not be mentioned in the *Democrat*. One day while checking marriage licenses in the courthouse, Aull noticed a note pinned to one of the entries. "Editors please omit," the note said. "By order of Bob himself. Death if violated." Aull explained to his readers: "After we read that we concluded that we would omit." And after a reader gave him the following tongue-lashing in 1910, he did change his candid approach regarding wedding announcements: "A woman likes to keep her marriage notices, and how do you think she'd like to let one of her grown daughters, twenty-five years hence, read where some fresh country editor called her 'buxom?' Say something that she can keep and at the same time save her face.

Your marriage notices are not for your readers. Remember that. They're one of the exclusive prerogatives of the bride."[75]

When a traveling evangelist shot the windows of the *Democrat* office full of holes one night in February 1911, Aull was more amused than angered. The preacher, a Rev. Tralle, had been giving a series of sermons on Christianity at the local Baptist Church. He told the congregation that he wouldn't spend a dollar with a merchant who wasn't a Christian. There were eight lawyers in town, he said, but only one did any sort of church work. And of the eighteen public school teachers in Lamar, only three were connected with the church and religious work. Aull was particularly interested in what Tralle had to say next:

> One of the most important things for a town, he declared, was clean newspapers, and Lamar was certainly woefully lacking here. The paper published upon the north side, the *Democrat,* he averred, was absolutely the worst he ever saw. He picked it up, the other day, and there was where a woman had sued her husband for a divorce and where the husband had blown his head off. It was infamous. Worse indeed than the yellowest yellow journal he had ever seen published in the cities. This paper should not be allowed to enter any Christian home. Personally, he had much rather a person would enter his kitchen and scatter a deadly poison in the food that was to be served his family, than for this paper to enter his house.[76]

After the sermon, Tralle mounted his horse and rode to the town square. As Aull described it, he proceeded to shoot "the whole *Democrat* office full of wintry starlight." Tralle reloaded his pistols and rode over to the east side of the square, where the *Lamar Republican-Sentinel* was located. He announced to those who had followed him from the church that this paper was not as bad as the *Democrat* but still had much room for improvement. Tralle then rode to the south side of the square, to the *Lamar Leader.* He fired a shot or two over the roof of the building and declared that the *Leader* was "the least bad of any in town." He encouraged his followers to take any job printing to the *Leader* and consider buying it to make it into a "good, clean paper."[77]

The few serious threats were not written up in the *Democrat,* largely because Aull didn't want to provoke any further violence. The *St. Louis Post-Dispatch* reported, many years after the fact, that in 1910 an irate farmer came to the *Democrat* to beat up Aull. Fortunately for the editor, he was out having a tooth extracted at the time. The farmer allegedly satisfied himself by beating up Aull's press foreman instead.[78]

Betty Aull White said she feared for her father's life three times during her childhood. "The Ku Klux Klan came marching down the street one night, carrying these burning torches, and said they were going to hang Arthur Aull," she said. The editor, wearing only a night shirt, dissuaded them from the window of an upstairs sleeping porch as the entire family watched. Another time, Aull angered some striking coal miners with his suggestion in the *Democrat* that they return to work. "I happened to be at the office for something," White remembered. "These men came up with a shotgun and said, 'Now we've got you, Arthur,' and shoved the shotgun at him. He called them 'damned fools' and told them to get out of there." The third occurrence was triggered by a story reporting that a woman's son had been jailed for public drunkenness. White recalled: "We were having dinner, the doorbell rang, and I went to the door. Here was this woman with a gun. I let out a shriek, and Dad came running up. He brought her into the house and talked to her. She said, 'I know he is a son of a bitch, but I don't like it in the paper.' "[79]

Only once was Aull actually assaulted. He milked the occasion for all it was worth, and the story eventually was reprinted as often as the Jennie Wirts episode. The trouble started in May 1943 when the *Democrat* reported that a Mrs. Brooks was circulating a petition urging marriage upon two disreputable people in her neighborhood. In a letter to Aull, Mrs. Brooks snapped: "I demand to know who the liar is. I intend to prosecute. Let me hear from you in the next five days. I aim to sue to [the] fullest extent of the law."[80] Two months later, Aull took a taxi to the neighborhood one Sunday morning, intending to interview Mrs. Brooks's friend for a follow-up. The friend, a Mrs. Eversall, immediately instructed her son to send for Mr. and Mrs. Brooks. According to Aull:

> The boy went out exclaiming and yelling for the Brookses to bring down the club and beat "him" up. Anyone with a whit of discretion would have seen by this time that he should be starting home. But since the matter of Mr. and Mrs. Brooks was coming up, it was, we felt, our place to stay and meet them. It wasn't long until Mrs. Brooks came. She was carrying a club in her hand about the length of a ball bat. It might not have been quite as heavy as a ball bat, but it was

plenty heavy. Of course there was nothing to do but stand our ground, but we must admit that we still didn't consider the matter too seriously. We certainly didn't believe Mrs. Brooks would use the club.[81]

Use the club she did, hitting Aull eight to ten times on the head and severing an artery in his forehead. The attack ended when Mr. Brooks arrived, but by this time Aull's shirt was covered with a mass of blood. He took a taxi home, and while he lay bleeding on a sofa awaiting a doctor, dictated the story to daughter Madeleine. "Fortunately we wore our old straw hat, which was some protection and we have a rather heavy head of hair which protected us some," the story concluded. "It would certainly have ruined a bald headed guy with no hat."[82]

LIBEL CHARGES

Aside from the criminal libel suits filed against him and two other Lamar editors in 1901 (see chapter 2), Aull was sued for libel only twice. Both cases were dismissed before coming to trial when the plaintiffs failed to file cost bonds of $250 and $200, respectively. He was represented by three of the finest attorneys in town, which may have discouraged additional libel suits on the part of disgruntled readers. Aull's attorneys included Edwin L. Moore, who, as the Barton County prosecuting attorney thirty years earlier, had filed a criminal libel charge against him.

The first case originated with a September 8, 1930, story reporting that Olive Kremp had divorced her husband, Walter. Aull hinted that the divorce was a conspiracy between the two, that Walter Kremp planned to sue the Barton County State Bank and would need her testimony that his bankruptcy had caused an alienation of her affections. Kremp brought suit against Aull and the Lamar Democrat Publishing Company for $10,000, claiming the story was "wilful, [sic] wanton and malicious." When Kremp failed to post the $250 cost bond to place the case on the circuit court docket, Judge Charles Hendricks dismissed it "with prejudice" in April 1931. When a case is dismissed with prejudice, it cannot be filed at a later date.[83]

The second libel case was over an article in the *Democrat* on September 25, 1934. Martha Lamar, the mother of a young man convicted of murder, brought a $50,000 suit against Aull and the Lamar Democrat Publishing Company for publishing "a certain false, scandalous and defamatory libel" about her. Earlier, in explaining the prosecutor's reason for recommending a parole for Lamar's son, Aull had pieced together a story that indicated the woman's lover may have been the actual murderer. He understandably was more shaken by this libel charge than the one four years earlier. Lamar and her husband also filed a notice with the Barton County recorder of deeds as a warning that if Aull sold the newspaper, the sale was subject to the provisions of the libel suit.[84]

The lawsuit weighed so heavily on his mind that he wrecked his yellow roadster on the town square the day after he heard he was being sued for $50,000. "Yours Truly in a Crash—When It Rains It Just Naturally Pours," read the headline in the *Democrat*. Aull, fearing that a libel conviction would put him out of business, breathed a sigh of relief when the plaintiff failed to raise the $200 cost bond. The case was dismissed in February 1935.[85]

AULL'S RISE TO PROMINENCE

Through newspaper exchanges with other publications across the state, the editor of the *Democrat* was widely known in Missouri early in his career. In those days, newspapers frequently reprinted interesting items from one another, giving credit to the originator. By 1911, Aull was already referring to himself as the regular "space filler" of the *Moberly Democrat,* well over two hundred miles away in north-central Missouri.[86] It took Harry Truman and syndicated columnist Ted Cook, though, to catapult Aull into national prominence.

As managing editor of the *Los Angeles Record* in the early 1920s, Cook originated a column that soon caught the eye of William Randolph Hearst. Cook was lured to the *Los Angeles Examiner* to write his humor column, "Cook-Coos," syndicated nationally beginning in 1928 by Hearst's King Features group. As one of the hundreds of columnists who sprang up in the 1920s trying to imitate the illustrious Walter Winchell, Cook struggled to find his niche. For months he read dozens of country papers searching for something strikingly new or unusual. He discussed his discovery in a 1938 interview with the *Missouri Press News:* "Finally, I realized I had discovered one paper, the Lamar Democrat, that completely held my interest. I read it through, day after day. I became interested in the happenings of the town. I discovered myself looking for certain names—names of people I had never seen. I soon felt I knew them."[87]

Cook started regularly reprinting items from the *Democrat* in his column. He found such gems as this one: "The Worthwhile Class gave their monthly party at the home of Miss Lela Richardson. Mrs. J. E. Hall read a magazine article: 'The Grave in the Garden.' This wasn't as gruesome as it sounds. The idea was that many cares and troubles found a grave in the garden if the care-burdened turned to the garden for solace. Miss Lela served popcorn and stick candy to the ladies."[88]

Cook's readers indicated that they were as fascinated with Lamar, Missouri, as he was. "Many of them, however, doubted that such a place existed," he said. "They hinted that they thought that I made up the items, which was not true." Cook may have had his doubts, though. Around 1933, he decided that he had to visit the town, the focal point of so many of his columns, and meet Arthur Aull. The columnist and his wife drove from California to Lamar, where someone pointed out the *Democrat* office. He described his first encounter with Aull: "Then I saw a gentleman with a white lawn tie sitting at a desk. He had classic features, dignified bearing. He wore a washable suit. I introduced myself. He looked me over with calm and obvious disappointment. Finally he said in a kindly voice: 'You and Mrs. Cook will come to my house. We'll have some supper. We will talk things over and you can rest here tonight.' "[89]

Cook said the evening he and his wife spent with the Aulls and their daughter Betty was one of the most interesting of his life: "Arthur Aull fairly bubbled with conclusions on every topic I could bring up. I found a scholar, an orator, an observer of life. I left next morning—but I was rather sorry to leave. I had the feeling that, for the first time in my life, my perspective toward small-town America was in focus. And I certainly had a new faith in the ability and wisdom of the small-town editor."[90]

The rise of Harry Truman, first as the Democratic nominee for vice president and later as the country's thirty-third president, also made Aull a national curiosity. The national media frequently turned up in Lamar in search of a human-interest piece about Truman's birthplace and more than once came away with a story about Aull instead. The town relished the national attention and did all it could to promote its connection to Truman. Lamar pulled a coup in 1944 by inviting the senator to kick off his campaign for the vice presidency in the town of his birth. Independence, Missouri, his longtime home, seemed a more logical choice, but Truman chose Lamar.

The ceremony in which Truman was officially notified that he was the Democratic nominee for vice president was held in Lamar on August 31, 1944. Seven bands played throughout the afternoon and evening as a crowd of about ten thousand awaited the arrival of Truman, eight other U.S. senators, and members of the state Democratic ticket. Truman's twenty-minute address was carried by the four major radio networks, making Lamar "the center of the eyes of the nation," as Aull put it.[91]

Margaret Truman wasn't nearly as impressed. The senator's daughter recalled in 1973 that the event was too much for a town the size of Lamar to handle. "Toilet facilities and the sewage system broke down," she wrote. "The parking field was turned into a huge mudhole by a heavy rainstorm the previous day." Aull, however, reported that the entire Truman Day went off without a hitch. "The day was made to order and everything moved merrily as a marriage bell," he wrote.[92]

Twelve days after the Truman ceremony, *Newsweek* became the first of the national magazines to make mention of Aull. In town to cover Truman's formal acceptance of the Democratic nomination, *Newsweek* discovered that Aull's efforts in blocking a nearby city's last-minute bid to wrest the rally from Lamar was more of a story. In describing him as a "free-thinking, free-speaking editor," *Newsweek* wrote, "The Lamar *Democrat*'s irrepressible editor, Arthur Aull, had laid bare Joplin's Machiavellian plans to 'steal the Truman show from Lamar, to keep all the big shots, the press agents, and the radio men in Joplin, bringing them up to Lamar a few minutes before the Truman speaking Thursday evening, where there would be a brief ceremony after which everyone would decamp to Joplin.' If that were true, Lamar told Democratic state leaders, 'just hold your darned meeting on some street corner in Joplin.' "[93]

Aull reprinted the entire *Newsweek* article in the *Democrat* under the headline "We Get Another Write-Up." Normally, though, he didn't share his "write-ups" with the folks in Lamar. When a reporter and a photographer from the *Chicago Daily News* spent two days following him around town in October 1943, he informed his readers of their visit but made no mention of the fact they were there for him.[94] Aull's most famous write-up, two pages in *Life* in 1945, was never mentioned in the *Democrat*. Neither was a 1946 piece in *Time*.

The *Life* article, headlined "Aull Prints All the News" and subtitled "Fearless Missouri editor gives the human touch," described his philosophy of newspapering and reprinted parts of three of the more unusual stories from the *Democrat*. "Unlike most country editors, whose papers reflect their own native caution and orthodoxy, Editor Aull believes it is his duty to tell literally everything that happens in his town," *Life* wrote. The much shorter *Time* article called his *Democrat* "one of the most widely quoted bush leaguers in the country" and "one of the last of the nation's free-spoken rural papers."[95]

Young Arthur Aull.
Courtesy of Betty Aull White.

Arthur Aull.
Courtesy of Betty Aull White.

Arthur Aull at his desk in the *Democrat* office. Courtesy of the *Lamar Democrat.*

Arthur Aull with daughter Betty on his shoulder. She said: "He would always walk up and down this long hallway in our house, during lunch, and do his thinking. He'd always say, 'Come on, Betts, let's write the editorial.' " Courtesy of Betty Aull White.

Arthur Aull and his dog Tippy outside the *Democrat* office, early 1940s. Courtesy of the *Lamar Democrat*.

Arthur Rozelle, shown here after leaving
Lamar, fought a vicious battle with Aull
in 1901 over legal advertising. Courtesy
of Alice Crockett Ladd.

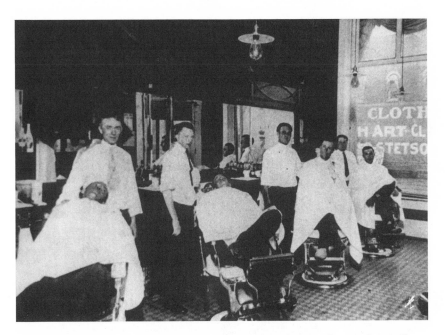

Will Jones's barber shop on the northwest corner of the square, where Arthur Aull
began every day with a shave. Jones is at the far left. Photo taken in 1908. Courtesy
of Bob Potter.

The southwest corner of the Lamar square, circa 1915. Aull led the campaign to pave the square in 1926. Courtesy of Bob Potter.

Barton County Sheriff John Harlow and his wife, Amanda. Harlow was shot and killed by Jay Lynch in a March 1919 jailbreak. Courtesy of Barton County Historical Society.

The body of Jay Lynch hangs in an elm tree on the lawn of the Barton County courthouse. Lynch was lynched on May 28, 1919, for the murder of Sheriff John Harlow and his son, Dick. Courtesy of Barton County Historical Society.

Harry Truman came to Lamar in August 1944 to accept the Democratic nomination for vice president. Courtesy of Bob Potter.

Luanna Aull, Genevieve Aull, and
Betty Aull (the baby). Courtesy of
Betty Aull White.

Luanna Aull (left) assumed the role of publisher upon Arthur
Aull's death, but day-to-day operation of the *Democrat* was left
to Madeleine (right) as the new editor. In this 1949 photo,
Luanna discusses a Western Union message with Madeleine.
Courtesy of the *Lamar Democrat*.

In this 1949 photo, Madeleine Aull Van Hafften looks over the latest edition of the *Democrat* as foreman Joe Roe stands by. Courtesy of the *Lamar Democrat.*

Madeleine Aull Van Hafften (left) and Luanna Aull in the *Democrat* office. Mrs. Aull served as publisher after the death of her husband. She died in 1968. Courtesy of the *Lamar Democrat.*

Madeleine Aull Van Hafften (left), Luanna Aull (center), and Betty Aull White (right) in 1954. Courtesy of Betty Aull White.

4

A LYNCHING IN
LAMAR

Any country editor can do what I am doing, but to avoid being lynched they'd better know their people pretty well before they start anything. I know and understand these people. I was reared with them. I'm one of them and I'm giving them what they want.

—*Arthur Aull, quoted in the* Kansas City Star, *June 6, 1937*

Arthur Aull made one notable exception to his all-the-news-is-fit-to-print philosophy. In 1919, when the people of Lamar and Barton County lynched a man for the murder of the popular sheriff and the sheriff's eighteen-year-old son, Aull refused to publish the names of the mob leaders. It was easily the most sensational story of his career, yet he stopped short of providing readers of the *Democrat* with all the facts.

The eruption of mob violence appalled Aull personally, but overwhelming community approval and concern for his own well-being dictated that he withhold the lynchers' identities. Most of Lamar already knew who had staged the mob execution, as one thousand men, women, and children celebrated the festive affair on the lawn of the Barton County courthouse. Publication of the leaders' names, however, likely would have resulted in their criminal prosecution and Aull's ostracism from the community.

The state of Missouri abolished capital punishment in 1917, sowing the seeds for future vigilantism. When a career criminal named Jay W.

Lynch shot and killed Barton County Sheriff John M. Harlow and fatally wounded his son, Dick, in a March 3, 1919, jailbreak, the people of Lamar clamored for vengeance rather than lawful justice. Lynch was captured in Colorado after a two-month manhunt and returned to Lamar for trial, where public sentiment was such that he not be allowed to escape alive. Lynch faced life imprisonment in the state penitentiary, but with the community cognizant of his three previous jail escapes and a flawed parole system that prematurely released convicted murderers, his fate was sealed.

PROFILES OF GOOD AND EVIL

In sixty-year-old John Harlow, the people of Lamar had the finest lawman to serve them since Wyatt Earp. A favorite of Republicans and Democrats alike, Harlow first was elected sheriff of Barton County in 1900. He served two two-year terms, then entered the real estate business before becoming town marshal in 1909. After a two-year stint as constable of the Lamar township, he was elected to a four-year term as sheriff in 1916.[1] Harlow and his wife, Amanda, had eight surviving children but only the one son, Dick, who, in a twist of fate, was shot in the same Barton County jail where he was born the day after his father was sworn in as sheriff the first time.[2]

The thirty-year-old Lynch, also known as George W. Owens, had been in and out of jail most of the decade. He was arrested in St. Louis in 1909 on three charges of burglary and sentenced to three years in the state reform school at Boonville, Missouri. He escaped, but was arrested nine months later in Kansas City for stealing sixty dollars' worth of rubber horse shoes. He was sentenced to two years in the state penitentiary but was paroled without serving any time.[3]

Lynch stole an automobile in Oklahoma City in November 1910 and three hundred dollars' worth of silks and women's clothing in Kansas City, Kansas, in May 1911. After pleading guilty to the robbery of a post office, he was fined a thousand dollars and sentenced to six months in jail. He escaped in October 1912, but was recaptured in April 1913 and given a suspended sentence for good behavior. In August 1913 he was apprehended in Denver and sentenced to nine to fourteen years in the Colorado State Penitentiary for highway robbery.

On August 30, 1916, he escaped from the warden's house, where he had been granted special privileges to work.[4]

Lynch was wanted in Buffalo, New York, for a burglary committed in September 1917. By 1918 he was working as a special detective for the Wabash Railroad in St. Louis, hired because of his skill with a gun. He was arrested in August 1918 for robbing a boxcar containing an interstate shipment. He was also suspected of counterfeiting. A friend signed a thousand-dollar bond for his release, and Lynch promptly jumped bail.[5]

SHERIFF HARLOW MURDERED

Lynch was arrested at his sister's farm home fourteen miles northwest of Lamar on Sunday afternoon, March 2, 1919, by four Barton County lawmen and turned over to Harlow at the Barton County jail. Harlow planned to take him by train the next day to St. Louis, where he was still wanted for the boxcar robbery. Lynch's mother, Maude, and his nineteen-year-old wife, Leola, visited him Monday morning, bringing two suitcases containing his belongings. The sheriff's wife, Amanda, searched the suitcases and found no weapons, but to her knowledge the suitcases were never passed to Lynch. The women asked to see Lynch, and Mrs. Harlow permitted them to talk to him through the bars at the back door of the jail. The prisoner's mother then said she had forgotten to bring along some of Lynch's personal papers that he would need in St. Louis. Mrs. Harlow finally agreed that Lynch's wife and infant daughter could go inside the jail and stay with him until Maude Lynch returned.[6]

Four hours later, she came back with a flat package wrapped in the comics section of the *Kansas City Post*. The package contained Lynch's memorandum book, some other papers, and, perhaps, the .45-caliber revolver that would be used by Lynch to murder Sheriff Harlow and his son. At about 7:30 P.M., shortly before Harlow and Lynch were to depart for St. Louis on the Missouri Pacific, Lynch asked to leave his cell to call his wife. As he stood at the telephone in a hallway between the dining room and the jail, he pulled out a pistol and shot the sheriff four times. Dick Harlow, who had just driven up to the jail and entered the dining room, was shot once at point-blank range as he went to the aid of his father. According to Mrs. Harlow, the sheriff gasped, "He's shot me, Mother. Good-bye and God bless you," before dying.[7]

Word of the murder spread quickly by telephone throughout Lamar and Barton County. Citizen posses were formed, and bloodhounds were brought in from Carthage and Springfield, Missouri. The dogs picked up a scent at the fairgrounds, and a large crowd roamed the area until 3 A.M. Tuesday, when it was assumed the fugitive had escaped in an automobile. Meanwhile, Lynch had spent the eight hours since his jailbreak running and walking through brush and briars, wading ditches and creeks, and climbing fences. Nearly exhausted and bleeding from numerous abrasions, he contemplated surrender when he found that his circuitous escape route had taken him back to Lamar and only a block away from his pursuers.[8]

Lynch headed out of town again, slipped and cut a bad gash in his leg, and finally took cover in a barn. He remained there for three days before following a nearby railway west through the towns of Iantha and Liberal. He came across another barn, covered himself with hay, and stayed there Friday and Saturday. By this point Lynch was famished; he hadn't eaten since his jailbreak Monday night. He summoned up enough strength to walk a few miles northwest to Oskaloosa, near the Kansas state line, where he boarded a freight train headed for Kansas City.[9]

Lynch made it to a suburb of Kansas City, where he caught a St. Louis-bound freight train. In St. Louis he took refuge at the home of an older woman whom he had known previously. He spent two weeks recovering in bed, reading newspaper accounts of his crime and the arrest of his mother and wife in connection with the shootings. Lynch somehow obtained a thousand dollars in cash before leaving St. Louis, then struck out for Springfield, Illinois. There he barely avoided capture when a man recognized him in a barbershop.[10]

Back in Lamar, hundreds of people turned out for the sheriff's funeral, with Aull noting, "To add to the bitter poignancy of the scene, Mrs. Harlow was led away from the church, weeping her heart out." She was unable to accompany the funeral procession to the cemetery because word was sent that her son's condition had worsened. He died a few days later, Lynch's bullet having severed his spinal cord. Aull, outraged as anyone in Lamar, helped fuel the community's fire: "It is hoped by every citizen in Barton County that this boy's death is not the final climax to this double shooting at the hands of an assassin. The climax should come with the capture of the man who fired the doubly murderous shots."[11]

LYNCH ARRESTED IN COLORADO

Following his near arrest in Illinois, Lynch set out for Arizona, where he intended to slip into Mexico. Unable to cross the Mexican border either by car or on foot, he went on to California before changing course for Colorado. He was arrested in La Junta, Colorado, on May 13, 1919, when an old acquaintance recognized him and informed local law officials. The new Barton County sheriff, Will Sewell, went to La Junta to pick him up, but Lynch had decided to fight the extradition to Missouri. He preferred a return to the Colorado State Penitentiary, from which he had escaped three years earlier. Lynch finally agreed to accompany Sewell back to Missouri once the sheriff consented that he would not be brought to Lamar and put on trial.[12] The prisoner later had a change of mind, however, and agreed to requests that his trial be held in Lamar.

On their return from Colorado, Lynch and Sewell were met in Kansas City by H. W. Timmonds, Barton County prosecuting attorney. They discussed taking Lynch to the state penitentiary in Jefferson City, but he begged them not to because of the dreadful prison food. It was decided that Lynch would be placed in the Bates County steel jail cell at Butler, Missouri, about fifty-five miles north of Lamar. There Sewell left orders that he not be permitted out of the cell and that no one else be allowed inside. The Bates County sheriff was given fifteen dollars of Lynch's money, because the prisoner insisted on purchasing his own food rather than eat jail fare.[13]

Sewell and Timmonds asked Lynch to sign a waiver forfeiting his right to ten days' notice before a special term of the circuit court could be held in Lamar. If Lynch agreed, he would be tried the next day. The prisoner inquired about the type of sentence he would receive, whether it would be life imprisonment or ninety-nine years. Another inmate who overheard the question asked what difference it made; Lynch would be dead regardless. Lynch insisted that the penitentiary would release someone who had served forty-two years of a ninety-nine-year sentence and that he might live to be seventy-two, thereby regaining his freedom. Lynch also asked about a change of venue, and Timmonds said he would not oppose it. But in the end, Lynch agreed to sign the waiver and come to Lamar if he would be allowed to talk with his wife for at least an hour after the trial.[14]

Despite repeated threats of mob violence if Lynch was brought to Lamar, local authorities devised a plan whereby he would be secretly whisked into town for an abbreviated trial in which a guilty plea was expected. Following sentencing, he would be taken by freight train to Nevada, Missouri, twenty-eight miles north, and then on to the state penitentiary. Sewell later told a *St. Louis Post-Dispatch* reporter: "For several days previous to the trial we had heard vague rumors of lynching, but knew of no organized effort to this end. I was prepared for the situation as well as could be in the circumstances."[15]

THE WORST-KEPT SECRET

Sewell, accompanied by the Bates County and Vernon County sheriffs and six deputies, brought Lynch to Lamar on Wednesday, May 28. Unknown to the nine lawmen, a telegram had been sent from Butler to Lamar telling of their departure on the Missouri Pacific. At the depot, several hundred people lined both sides of the track awaiting the train's arrival. Aull noted that "by one o'clock a line of autos was dashing down to Pacific street to the station. There was a suppressed air of excitement, apparent in the demeanor of every one you met."[16]

The train, scheduled to pull in at 1:18, was about forty-five minutes late. Lynch was taken from the rear of the back coach, hurried into Prosecutor Timmonds' car, and driven to the courthouse. The *Kansas City Times* later reported that fifty men waited at the south entrance to the courthouse to seize Lynch upon his arrival but abandoned their plan when the train was late. Inside the courthouse, the circuit courtroom quickly filled. Aull, who hurriedly made the drive from the train station to the courthouse, noted: "At first the people trickled in, so you could count them. Soon the crowd poured in, like a torrent, filling every corner, all of them standing up, craning their necks, for the first glimpse of Lynch."[17]

Aull met the outlaw, face to face, when Sewell and his deputies marched him up to the courtroom from the first-floor sheriff's office. He described him as "a larger, heavier man, than his lithographs indicate. His frontal view is not bad. His profile is suggestive of the sneering and the sinister." Lynch displayed the characteristics of a gentleman rather than a notorious killer. He wore a dark green Stetson hat and a blue serge suit, and his collar was neatly laundered. When the lawmen came for him that morning at the Bates County jail, he expressed his disappointment over their failure to bring him his silk shirt. He was clean shaven, with "his hair combed until a fly would have slipped on it."[18] As he entered the courtroom, he removed his hat with his manacled hands.

Lynch was taken into Judge B. G. Thurman's office for a few minutes, then brought out when the judge arrived. The jury was in its box, having entered secretly. The authorities, who considered calling the trial off, were relieved when onlookers did not appear uncontrollable. Thurman later told the Associated Press, "The courtroom was filled with people, but there were many women and children, and it seemed a crowd attracted simply by curiosity."[19]

As the trial began, it was evident that things were being rushed. Prosecutor Timmonds hurriedly read the indictment against Lynch, who listened calmly. Thurman asked Lynch to stand and answer the charges, and he replied, "Guilty." Thurman then asked Lynch if he had anything to say, if there was any reason why he should not be sentenced for the murders of John and Dick Harlow. When Lynch shook his head and said "No," Thurman sentenced him to life imprisonment.[20]

Thurman, now in no hurry to speed up the proceedings, took about five minutes to admonish Lynch for the career path he had chosen. Had the prisoner used his talents of great nerve and determination, Thurman said, he would have already risen to a position of greater prominence than anyone present in the courtroom. He reminded Lynch that it was never too late to change one's ways and said he hoped he would use his time in prison to do good rather than evil.[21]

Thurman also directed his message to those in the crowd, advising that they must not allow their zeal for justice to subvert the law. Any violence toward Lynch, he said, would not bring Sheriff Harlow back. He asked them to prove to the world that they were law-abiding citizens and permit the law to run its course. They need not fear that Lynch would again escape from jail, he said. Aull recorded Lynch's response: "I want to say to you, your honor, that I had no intention, in the beginning, of killing Sheriff Harlow. As for his son, it was an accident. I did not know that I killed him. No man regrets it more than I."[22]

An uneasy stillness now fell over the jammed courtroom. No one dared to leave, in the event that what had been talked about for weeks might actually occur. After Sewell and his deputies had directed Lynch back into the judge's private chambers, a voice in the crowd yelled "String him up!" The sheriff quickly took charge of the situation, saying another outburst like that one would land the speaker in jail. With that, the crowd started filing out of the courtroom. F. D. W. Arnold, owner and publisher of the *Lamar Republican-Sentinel,* felt confident enough that mob violence had been averted that he returned to his office to write the account of Lynch's trial. The final paragraph of his story similarly reflected the attitude of the nine lawmen who had relaxed their guard: "At this writing Lynch is still in the southeast room with the officers. Naturally feeling is somewhat high, but the crowd's curiosity has been somewhat satisfied, and it is thinning out. The people have seen the man they have long wanted to look upon, and we feel pretty sure the officers will so perform their duty that Lynch will leave this evening for his new home at Jefferson City, where we fervently hope he remains until the sentence of Judge Thurman has been fully carried out."[23]

Lynch, still in Thurman's chambers, asked to see his wife, Leola, and five-month-old daughter after a brief visit with his mother. Sewell recommended they leave immediately for the depot where the freight train was waiting, but kept his promise to give Lynch some time with his family. Sewell then removed the prisoner's handcuffs so that he might hold his daughter. Lynch kissed the baby several times and implored his wife to give the child an education.[24]

LYNCH IS SEIZED

A crowd of about one thousand that included the editor of the *Democrat* amassed outside the courthouse a few minutes after Lynch had been sentenced to life imprisonment. Unlike his counterpart at the *Republican-Sentinel,* Aull had not returned to his office but had remained in the thick of the impending lynching party. He noted a "mob spirit [that] kindled and flared," as the crowd stood gazing up toward the windows of the room where Lynch was. The prisoner, he said, "remained up there in the death trap, like a rat, waiting to be thrown to a pack of terriers."[25]

At 3:40 P.M. a "blood curdling shout" went up from the crowd as a group of about fifty men, led by a prominent Lamar businessman, rushed into the courthouse. One of the men carried a small suitcase, the contents of which were known to everyone. The neck-tie party poured into the courtroom and forced open the door to the judge's chambers. Sewell drew his revolver and threatened to kill the first person who advanced. He gave the following account to a *St. Louis Post-Dispatch* reporter: "I was standing, my back to the door, and near the jury box, when two men rose from the jury box and pinioned my arms, pulling me over the rail. They were a blacksmith and a liveryman. I struggled to free myself, when others pounced upon me and pushed me back in the room. Lynch quickly passed the child to his wife when the mob seized him. She fainted in the arms of Deputy Sheriff Stonum. A merchant had a rope, which he threw over Lynch's neck."[26]

The mob dragged Lynch headfirst over the banister and chairs in the courtroom and down three short flights of steps to the first floor of the courthouse. By this time the prisoner likely was dead, either from a broken neck, strangulation, or a fractured skull. Sewell's wife and friends, fearing for his safety, restrained him from going downstairs after the lynching party. The sheriff recognized two farmers, two former soldiers, a threshing machine operator, and an employee of a bottling company among the lynchers who overpowered him.[27]

The mob let out a "vociferous yell" as it emerged from the courthouse pulling Lynch's lifeless body on a rope. "Women joined in the howling," reported the *Kansas City Times*. "It was a gala day for Lamar." Lynch was dragged down the north steps of the courthouse and across the lawn to a small elm tree just a short distance north of the window of the sheriff's office.[28] Ironically, John Harlow had planted the tree about fifteen years earlier, during his first stint as sheriff of Barton County.

A young man, reportedly a soldier who had served in World War I, climbed the elm and placed the rope over a small limb. But the rope slipped off and had to be thrown up to the man again. This time it was placed nearer the tree's truck, and a dozen men hoisted Lynch's body into the air. The crowd was quiet at first, then some voiced their approval. One older man said the same fate should befall the state legislators who had voted to abolish capital punishment two years earlier. Amanda Harlow, wife of the late sheriff, watched the lynching with several of her daughters from a car parked at the side of the courthouse square. It was her first public appearance since the funeral of her son, Dick.[29]

Women, many carrying babies, jostled with the men for better vantage points. Children stood under the elm and gazed wide-eyed at the spectacle, some trying to touch Lynch's feet. Others pulled leaves off the tree and carried them away as souvenirs.[30] Eleven-year-old Betty Aull, however, missed Lamar's holiday affair:

> I was way out on my bicycle, visiting a friend. My mother called and said, "Betty, I want you to come right home. This is the way you're to come home. If you don't follow it exactly, you're going to get the worst spanking you've ever gotten in your life." Of course, she was having me miss the square; we didn't live too far from there. When I got home she said to get in the house and stay in the house. After Dad got home, he talked about it. I wanted to know what "lynch" meant. So he very carefully explained lynching to me.[31]

Soon after Lynch was hanged, the crowd began murmuring that Maude and Stella Lynch should meet with the same fate. His mother was still awaiting trial on the charge of supplying the revolver used to kill the Harlows, and his sister had outraged those still present in the courtroom after the trial with her denunciation of Prosecutor Timmonds, Sheriff Sewell, and one of her mother's attorneys. The mob searched for Maude and Stella Lynch, but they were concealed in the office of Maude Lynch's attorneys, from where they watched the lynching across the square. The attorneys asked Sewell to allow the two women to spend the night in the Lamar jail, but he adamantly refused, saying: "There has been enough hanging in this town today. I don't want any more. The crowd is still crazy and will string them up, if they stay in town, and their location leaks out."[32] The women were taken by the Vernon County sheriff to his jail in Nevada, Missouri, where they safely spent the night.

Leola Lynch, who had fainted when the lynchers seized her husband, did not regain consciousness until two hours later at the home of Sheriff Sewell and his wife. She remained in a dazed condition until midnight, when she asked Mrs. Sewell where her husband was. Leola Lynch and her infant daughter spent the night with the Sewells, at the Lamar jail, then left by train the next morning for Joplin, Missouri.[33]

Lynch's body hung in the tree for two hours until Sewell ordered it cut down at 5:50 P.M. He said he would have removed it sooner but was told by the crowd to leave it alone. No attempt had been made to mutilate the body, which often occurred after a lynching. The publisher of the *Lamar Republican-Sentinel* pointed out a curious feature: Lynch's hair "remained parted nearly as neatly as when he stood in the courtroom before Judge Thurman."[34]

Lynch's body was carried to a local mortuary for the night, then taken by train to Joplin the next morning. In Joplin, a large crowd waited for the train, which also contained Lynch's wife, daughter, mother, and sister. Several hundred people viewed the body at the funeral home there before the Lynch family requested that no more onlookers be admitted. J. W. Lynch, the deceased's father, drove the family to Kansas City before the 6 P.M. burial. Only five men attended the brief service at Forest Park Cemetery in Joplin—two undertakers, a local Methodist minister, a reporter, and a friend of Lynch's from Chanute, Kansas. The minister gave a short talk titled "The wages of sin is death."[35]

GOVERNOR DEMANDS ACTION

Coroner J. C. Harmon, who cut down the body, did not conduct an inquest the night of the lynching on the advice of Prosecutor Timmonds. Many who had witnessed the spectacle gathered in small groups on street corners throughout the evening, and Timmonds did not want to further provoke the mob. The next morning, he and Sewell began a quiet investigation. He promised a vigorous prosecution, but told a *Kansas City Times* reporter: "We are finding great difficulty in obtaining tangible information. Until the mob spirit dies down and the pendulum swings toward rationalism and sane thought, little can be done."[36]

Sewell, as expected, could identify practically all of the lynchers, and, in fact, had called many of them by name in the courthouse fight to seize Lynch. He said there were about twenty men he would classify as "ringleaders" but would not reveal their identities unless ordered to do so on the witness stand. Timmonds, who was in his office across the street from the courthouse when the mob snatched Lynch, said he did see the man who climbed the elm tree with the rope. But his investigation was nearing an impasse. "Some of my best friends have told me that they would rot in jail before they divulged the name of any one in the mob," he said.[37]

Missouri Governor Frederick Gardner, surprised that Barton County authorities had not kept him apprised of the lynching and ensuing investigation, sent a telegram to Timmonds the next evening demanding information: "What are [the] facts and what action is contemplated? Do you desire assistance of [the] attorney general in an investigation and in the prosecutions which may follow?" Gardner said he would wait only a short time for Barton County to take action before ordering an official inquiry through the state's attorney general.[38]

But short of calling out the National Guard, there was little a governor could do. Lynchings were not uncommon. Missouri averaged slightly more than two per year from 1882 to 1937, ranking it twelfth among the states. In 1919 alone, there were eighty-three lynchings in the United States. While lynchings were usually acts of racial violence, that was not the situation in Lamar. Lynch was one of only four white men hanged by a mob in 1919. A further difficulty in prosecuting those involved was that Missouri had no antilynching legislation. The law only provided that a sheriff may employ sufficient guards to protect his prisoner or move that prisoner to a jail in another county for safekeeping.[39] Sewell had followed both courses of action before bringing Lynch to Lamar.

METROPOLITAN PRESS DENOUNCES LAMAR

Hundreds of newspapers, including the *New York Times,* published accounts of Jay Lynch's execution.[40] Nearly every major newspaper in Missouri editorialized on the lynching, the majority condemning the people of Lamar for taking the law into their own hands. Others demanded that Governor Gardner and the authorities of Barton County seek out and punish those responsible. The most vehement disapproval of Lamar's mob execution came from the *Kansas City Post,* which drew a correlation between the lynching and the recent Bolshevik seizure of power in Russia:

> Lawlessness has once more replaced law and order in Missouri and the swift, terrible, degrading blood lust of lynch law blots the fair name of the state.
>
> A community, one of the best in the state, goes berserker with rage and exhibits all the attributes of a Russian mob.
>
> That men who are ordinarily good citizens banded themselves to-

gether, entered the very temple of justice and dragged forth a man who had been given the extreme penalty of the law and then deliberately murdered him while a crowd of men and women applauded, is not a spectacle upon which the state may look with either pride or tolerance.

Lynchings are a defiance of all law and those who engage in them brand themselves as outlaws. It is a return to the jungle and the ethics of the cave. It is anarchy, triumphant and brutal. It is bolshevism at its worst.[41]

The *St. Louis Post-Dispatch* conceded that the Lamar incident lacked two of the usual unsavory features of lynchings—there was no doubt about the prisoner's guilt, and there was no additional brutality—but considered the mob's crime more grievous than Lynch's. "It was an attack on all law and order, an attempt to subvert them and to substitute personal vengeance for justice under legal process, and mobs for courts," the paper stated, urging that those responsible be indicted and punished.[42]

An article in one of Aull's rival newspapers, the *Oskaloosa* (Mo.) *News,* gleefully pointed out that Lamar would hereafter be known as "the place where Lynch was hanged." The alliteration of "Lynch and Lamar" would haunt the town, the article said, until a future generation had forgotten its significance. The *News* also attacked the newspapers of Lamar for their failure to denounce the mob action, claiming future historians would wonder whether it was due to sympathy or policy.[43]

One metropolitan paper, the *St. Louis Star,* was sympathetic to Lamar and laid the blame at the feet of the penal system itself. In a bit of investigative reporting, the *Star* discovered that 238 convicted murderers had been paroled from the state penitentiary during the previous five years. Some serving life sentences had spent as little as seven years behind bars. "A sentence of life imprisonment, pronounced with the gravest solemnity, oftentimes means freedom for the prisoner after a few years' confinement," the *Star* editorialized. "Court sentences, which in theory should rid the community of dangerous characters, have been made farcical."[44] The *Star* urged Governor Gardner to reform the parole system in Missouri rather than focusing his attention on the lynchers in Lamar.

Many of the country papers were also kind to Lamar. Tom Bodine,

editor of the *Paris* (Mo.) *Mercury,* wrote that Lynch had gunned down
Sheriff Harlow and his son as "wantonly and as deliberately as he would
have killed a dog, with as little feeling and absolutely no compunction."
Since Lynch was not hanged until he had confessed his crime in court
and had received a "life" sentence of about ten years, the people of
Lamar were justified in protecting themselves in the only way possible
against the "growing tribe of professional killers," Bodine said.[45]

C. L. Hobart, editor of the *Holden* (Mo.) *Progress,* blasted the metropolitan press for condemning the community while condoning the conduct of gangsters in their cities. The people of Lamar, he wrote, had
grown tired of the "machinations of shyster lawyers, farcical jurors, stul-
tified witnesses, sycophantic judges and venal pardon officials, all of
which are rapidly making what we call the 'law' a joke." Because it had
taken the law into its own hands, the community had forever protected
itself from a "vicious degenerate, a menace to society."[46]

Support also came from an unexpected source. The *Democrat* received a letter to the editor from an unidentified man in Kansas City
who claimed 95 percent of that city's inhabitants were saying "Hurrah
for Lamar." Aull normally followed a strict policy of rejecting unsigned
letters, but made an exception in this instance: "Allow Kansas City to
congratulate the good citizens of Lamar for their noble act this week in
bringing to [a] close the low down life of Jay Lynch. A more noble deed
in my estimation could not be done and the pluck and bravery together
with the desire for justice in those citizens are admired by every citizen
of Kansas City."[47]

AULL'S PERSPECTIVE

As a bystander outside the courthouse before the lynching, Aull observed the leaders of the mob assembling moments before Lynch was
seized. One man carried the suitcase that contained the rope; another
pointed to the elm, bringing a nod of approval from the rest. Rather
than hastening inside to warn Sheriff Sewell and the others, Aull remained among the crowd awaiting the inevitable. While he expected a
lynching, he was not prepared for the barbarity of the reality. He later
wrote that he could not visualize "the sinister, ghastly and terrible features of the hanging, until it actually occurred." He likened the sordid

affair to "having a crowd catch a mad dog, drag him into your house and butcher him."[48]

Aull undoubtedly knew the names of all the members of the lynching party. They were his friends, neighbors, and fellow businessmen. But in his most significant departure from established procedure, he neglected to provide readers of the *Democrat* with all the facts. Of course, most of his local readers already knew the identities of the nine or so ringleaders. But the *Democrat*'s circulation extended far beyond Lamar and Barton County. In this instance, Aull's readership included Governor Gardner, Attorney General Frank McAllister, and C. P. LeMire, the assistant attorney general sent to the community to investigate the lynching.

LeMire spent a frustrating day in Lamar on June 9, twelve days after the lynching, interviewing numerous residents who had witnessed the crime. As he walked around the square, he was astonished that no one could single out anyone involved. One person did recall that the man who climbed the elm was barefooted, but he could not further identify him.[49] Had Aull published the names of the lynchers, the attorney general's office might have made a case for prosecution.

But Aull, a keen judge of public sentiment, quickly realized that the hanging of Jay Lynch had the approval of nearly the entire community. About two hours after the lynching, while the body still swung from the tree, a "leading citizen . . . a strict church member" advised Aull to take it easy on the community in writing the story. Other "serious minded" church members told him of their approval of the lynching. An eminent Barton Countian, after Lynch met his death, said to Aull, "Gosh, I was so darned afraid he'd get out of town alive, I didn't know what to do."[50]

In Lamar, the only substantial opposition to the lynching came from the local Methodist pastor. In a Sunday sermon eighteen days after the hanging, the Rev. Waters denounced it as an act of "brutal lawlessness." He told the congregation: "That lynching was done by men you wouldn't allow to come into your houses. Yet you openly sympathized with them if you did not aid them."[51]

As for a precedent, Aull recalled the only other time a man had been lynched in Lamar. In 1892, when Aull was nineteen, a farmhand named Robert Hepler was hanged by a mob for the brutal murder of a woman and her five-year-old son. A mob of about one hundred men assembled in Lamar, took a train to Nevada, Missouri, where Hepler had been transferred for his own safety, and seized the prisoner.[52] He was taken back to Lamar and strung up in an elm tree near the spot where Lynch would be hanged twenty-seven years later. The *Democrat* failed to identify any of the lynching party.

Aull, like the previous editor of the *Democrat* and the nine lawmen armed to protect Lynch, bowed to community insistence that nothing be done to tarnish the reputations of those who had done the lynching. Although Sheriff Sewell was overpowered by the mob and stripped of his revolver, his deputies fired not a single shot that day in 1919. Those who believed the authorities were derelict in their duties were reminded of the following by Aull: "If an officer had shot down a local man, in defense of Lynch, if he had not been torn limb from limb, right there on the spot, he never could have lived among these people. The load of odium and hatred that would have been his, for months to come, would have been more than any man could bear."[53]

Aull was not alone in his decision to play down the local and state investigation into the lynching. In his study of southern country newspapers from 1865 to 1930, Thomas Clark contended that rural editors, as community spokesmen, might have been more vigorous in publicly identifying lynching participants. This information was easily obtainable, he claimed, noting that few editors made any effort to tone down the lurid details of a lynching. Clark, though, said country editors were timid as a rule, and perhaps it was unfair to ask them to announce the names of mob participants: "There was, of course, constant danger of physical injury and libel suits, but the publication of names of even the leaders of mobs would have had a highly chastening influence. In all honesty, it was too much to ask the earlier Southern country editor to take a bold and highly unpopular stand in a field where sheriffs, coroners juries, grand juries, prosecuting attorneys, church leaders and courts were unwilling to crusade for the fight."[54]

Those in a community who disapproved of a lynching would withhold information for fear of ostracism or personal safety, according to James McGovern, who conducted a case study of a black man lynched in Florida in 1934. McGovern found that community approval legitimated the astounding number of lynchings in rural America. This approval was either explicit, in the form of widespread participation by the community, or implicit, in the form of acquittal of the mob with or without a trial. Lamar exhibited both types of approval, as well as two other forms of approbation that McGovern identified: a manhunt and display of the victim's body in a prominent place.[55]

CAPITAL PUNISHMENT RESTORED

Due in large part to the Lamar lynching, the Missouri General Assembly restored capital punishment in an extra session six weeks after Jay Lynch's execution. Stirred by a speech from Representative H. C. Chancellor of Barton County, the Missouri House of Representatives voted 87 to 19 to repeal the 1917 act that abolished the death penalty. Opposition came from the Woman's Christian Temperance Union, which dispatched a telegram read on the house floor shortly before the vote was taken at 12:30 A.M. In the state senate, the bill passed 18 to 2. Hours later, Governor Gardner officially signed into law the restoration of capital punishment (hanging) for seven crimes—treason, perjury, subornation of perjury, first-degree murder, rape, kidnapping, and train robbing.[56]

Back in Barton County, Judge Thurman charged a grand jury with investigating the lynching and returning indictments if sufficient evidence existed to prosecute any of the mob members. Thurman said a murder had been committed at the courthouse and that he considered it a "gross act of lawlessness," regardless of Lynch's criminal past. It was a grand jury that no one wanted to serve on; five of the members appointed by the county court pleaded with Thurman to be dismissed but were turned down. The grand jury interviewed several witnesses, including some with "first hand and first rope knowledge," but could not obtain any tangible evidence. Aull's story on the grand jury's report dripped with sarcasm: "But apparently the boys were all so flustered and excited, at the time, that they can't remember just what they did see. They have a dim, shadowy impression that Jay Lynch in someway got his neck into a halter and pulled himself up a tree, but just how he did it, they don't exactly know."[57]

Maude Lynch, the deceased's mother, was tried twice on the charge of furnishing the gun used to kill Sheriff Harlow and his son. The first trial, moved from Lamar for fear of another lynching, ended in a hung jury. When her failing health delayed a second trial for several months, Aull urged that the case be dismissed. Calling her a "broken woman," he argued that her days were numbered and that she had already suffered more than her son. But a retrial was held, and in June 1920, more than a year after the lynching, Maude Lynch was acquitted. Two surprise witnesses, a pair of county court judges, testified that a corner of the screen over one of the jail windows had been pried loose.[58] In the eyes of the jury, an accomplice other than his mother may have slipped Lynch the murder weapon.

As his community's most influential spokesman, Aull might have prevented the murder of Jay Lynch by waging a crusade against lynch law soon after Lynch's capture. Or, he could have used his skills as a public speaker to denounce the expected mob action when the crowd of one thousand gathered outside the courthouse. Yet he took no steps to dissuade a premeditated act of violence. Departing from his usual policy of providing editorial leadership, he preferred to remain a bystander. In this instance the community would not have tolerated a contrary viewpoint from an insider. Aull provided comprehensive coverage of Jay Lynch's getaway, capture, and trial, but few details of the resulting investigation. What little editorial comment he did offer on the lynching sidestepped the question of whether the people of Lamar were justified in hanging Lynch. He wrote: "Understand, we're not saying the crowd did right, just now, or that it did wrong. We're just telling what we know are the facts. . . . The lynching was done. Let's not undertake to lie about it. The truth is always best in the end. If evils exist they can only be remedied, by first knowing the truth."[59]

5

SURVIVAL OF THE

FITTEST

The newspaper is run by a business man, no more concerned materially with political victories and defeats than the proprietor of the town's leading ready to wear store. He learns what the people want to read, supplies it to them, builds up his subscription list and furnishes the advertisers a real chance to get their wares before prospective buyers.

—Arthur Aull, June 27, 1929

The life of a country newspaper editor was full of hardships. Depressed economic conditions, skilled labor shortages, delinquent advertisers and subscribers, constant equipment failures, and competition from other papers all added up to meager profit margins and often bitter struggles for existence. With the exception of such notables as Ed Howe, William Allen White, and Henry Beetle Hough, most country editors labored in near obscurity. They were influential men in their own communities, but few received any type of regional or national acclaim.

The work wasn't backbreaking, but the hours were long. A 1911 survey conducted by the University of Kansas found that country editors in that state worked fourteen to fifteen hours per day seven days a week. Only one-sixth of their time was spent gathering and writing the news; the remaining time was devoted to soliciting job work and advertising, setting type, and running the presses.[1]

A few country editors who managed to find time to write for outside audiences built national reputations on their literary works. Ed Howe, editor of the *Atchison* (Kans.) *Globe* from 1877 to 1910, wrote *The Story of a Country Town* (1882) and articles for the *Saturday Evening Post* and other widely read magazines. William Allen White, editor of the *Emporia* (Kans.) *Gazette* from 1895 to 1944, wrote *In Our Town* (1906), *A Certain Rich Man* (1937), and his autobiography (1946) along with numerous opinion pieces for magazines of national circulation. Henry Beetle Hough, editor of the *Vineyard Gazette,* on Martha's Vineyard Island, published a number of books, including the classic *Country Editor* (1940).

Any free time Arthur Aull had went back into the *Democrat.* Bored with a weekly, he converted the newspaper to daily publication within a year of its purchase. He then devoted his energies to getting payment on past-due subscriptions, upgrading the equipment and facilities, cultivating new advertisers, and boosting the newspaper's lagging circulation. It was at the latter task that he proved to be the most successful; the readership of the *Democrat* more than tripled thanks to subscription contests in 1909 and 1911.

Unlike the country editors in the 1911 University of Kansas study, Aull spent an inordinate amount of time gathering and writing the news of his community. After his death in 1948, a friend estimated that Aull had written eighty-five million words—about five thousand per day—as editor of the *Democrat.*[2] His writing style caught the eye of the J. Walter Thompson advertising agency, which offered Aull the opportunity to star on his own radio program in New York. But his age (sixty-eight), coupled with his love of his community and the allegiance he felt toward it, caused him to turn down the chance for immediate stardom.

TREADING WATER

N. W. Ayer and Son's Directory estimated the *Democrat's* circulation at fifteen hundred when Aull took over the newspaper in August 1900. He figured the circulation to be closer to five hundred. In an attempt to get a grip on the *Democrat's* readership, the new editor sent statements to those subscribers who had failed to make a payment since his purchase of the newspaper. Christmas 1900 was but three weeks away, and the young editor's own bills were mounting. Wary of insulting the *Democrat's* readers, however, Aull cautioned, "If you can't pay of course it can't be helped, but help us out if you can. Don't fly off the handle and say you are dunned and insulted, for these statements contain nothing to offend anyone."[3]

Every December Aull made a plea for the *Democrat's* delinquent subscribers to come to the office before the first of the year and settle their accounts. Polite notes were sent to those a year or more in arrears, but even then he was cautious of offending anyone. "If you shouldn't happen to have the money, keep in a good humor and wait until you get it and then remember us," he wrote in 1902. In 1908, when postal inspectors started examining the subscription lists of country newspapers to validate second-class mailing permits, Aull warned that delinquent readers "will be subjected to the humiliation of having their name marked off, and placed in a dead list for outside collection." And if that threat failed, Aull reminded subscribers, "We need some new shingles on the house, and b'gosh, we ain't yet got our winter's underwear."[4]

Readers of the *Democrat* were getting a good deal for a dollar a year, Aull thought, and he told them so every issue:

> The *Democrat* is conceded on all hands to be Southwest Missouri's best and brightest local newspaper. Tell your neighbor about it, if he is not one of its readers.
> The *Democrat* is the most closely read paper in the county. Its advertising columns give the best results. It is patronized by the live merchants and read by the progressive and enterprising people.
> The *Democrat* prints more local news than any other paper ever published in Lamar. It is a paper of opinions and it is not afraid to express them. Once form the habit of reading it and you will wonder how you ever got along without it.[5]

Despite Aull's efforts at self-promotion, the *Democrat's* circulation continued to trail the two other newspapers in Lamar. By 1909, his old nemesis, the *Leader,* was claiming sixteen hundred readers for its weekly edition and four hundred for its daily. By comparison, the *Democrat* reported one thousand weekly subscribers and three hundred daily subscribers, while the *Republican-Sentinel,* a weekly, announced a readership of nineteen hundred.[6]

A NEW HOME

Improvements to the newspaper, including a new job press and "practically new machinery all around," served to plunge Aull only deeper in debt. He announced early in 1909 that the "re-equipment" of the *Democrat*'s office had cost more than three thousand dollars. He incurred even more expense in finding a new home for his paper when the county court requested that it vacate its office in the courthouse. Aull had mixed emotions about leaving the west half of the courthouse basement, where the *Democrat* had been for nineteen years. The farewell messages, rhymes, and other bits of wisdom left by his predecessors on the dark and grimy walls of the office inspired him and provided a sense of tradition. But the basement was extremely cold in the winter, and Aull had grown tired of locals calling him the "long-haired man in the cellar," "the courthouse rat," and "the ring organ in the basement." The county court had also steadily raised his rent, from $115 a year to $240.[7]

Aull arranged to have a building erected north of the courthouse, on the square, where a meat market once stood. That stone-fronted building on Tenth Street would be home to the *Democrat* for the next seventy-seven years. The paper's move completed, Aull tackled the problem of boosting his sagging readership. In the fall of 1909 he launched the first of two subscription drives that more than tripled the *Democrat*'s circulation but ultimately landed him back in circuit court.

THE PIANO CONTEST

Aull purchased an elaborate mahogany-cased piano for four hundred dollars from the Rhodes Music Company of Lamar to award to "the young woman in Barton county" who accumulated the most points in the *Democrat*'s subscription contest. Contestants would receive six hundred points for selling a new, one-year subscription to the weekly *Democrat* and fifty points for every dollar paid upon an existing subscription account. The contest was to close at midnight on New Year's Day, 1910.[8]

Six serious contenders for the piano quickly emerged, all enlisting the aid of friends and relatives to support their campaigns. Only fifty points separated Bessie Bartlett, a young Barton County teacher, and twelve-year-old Nina Adams as the contest entered its final week. Adams's grandfather, Judge J. M. Nowlin, nearly won the piano for her single-handedly by obtaining more subscriptions "than any other half dozen workers upon either side."[9] Bartlett divided her contingent of helpers into two groups, one out in the western part of the county and one in Lamar.

Subscriptions to the *Democrat* poured in on the contest's final day. Townspeople were nearly evenly divided in their support of Adams and Bartlett, although many rooted for the latter near the end because she appeared to be losing the contest. However, the seeming gap closed considerably when Bartlett's workers from outside Lamar arrived late in the evening with a large number of subscriptions. Aull wasn't keeping a running total of the points, but presumed Adams was winning.[10]

The two rivals and their friends awaited the opening of the ballot box at midnight in the *Democrat* office. It took more than an hour for all the points to be tallied by County Recorder John Pahlow and an assistant. Finally, it was announced that Bartlett had 170,050 points, Adams 148,500. The winner thanked her friends for the work they had done, and the crowd that had gathered to witness the end of the contest cheered her heartily.[11]

It mattered little to Aull who won the contest; the *Democrat* was the ultimate victor. The six contestants had accumulated 370,000 points, which translated into hundreds of new subscribers for the newspaper and more than a thousand dollars in Aull's pocket. More importantly, a larger number of the new subscribers were Republicans, a fact not lost on the shrewd editor. Aull believed he had broken down the last barrier—politics—to the *Democrat* becoming the dominant paper in Lamar and Barton County. The new Republican readers, he said, "will soon learn that they have subscribed for a paper that has neither an ax to grind nor a grouch, and most of them will be glad to renew, when their time expires."[12]

But in entering the new subscribers' names on the books, Aull discovered that Bartlett's actual point total was some sixty thousand less than the sum of her tickets in the ballot box. He determined that the *Democrat* had not issued about a hundred of the tickets, each worth six hundred points, to the teacher or her friends. The mortified Aull later reflected that for the next several days he "dreamed piano, ate piano, had piano between meals, and our evening's entertainment was piano, piano, piano."[13] He decided to investigate further and then discuss the situation with Bartlett, hoping she would relinquish her claim to the piano after learning that thousands of points had been wrongfully credited to her total. Meanwhile, the piano remained at the Rhodes Music Company's store near the *Democrat* office.

Aull elected to go ahead and publish the results of the contest, announcing Bartlett as the winner, two days after the fiasco. But he continued his private inquest, visiting the home of a young man named Elmer Poague who had been observed the night of the contest carrying a wad of piano tickets. Poague's parents told Aull that an inebriated Elmer had helped stuff the ballot box and, at that very moment, was in town wanting to confess to the editor of the *Democrat*. Aull hurried back to Lamar and found Poague, who admitted that at the urging of Bartlett's father and fiancé he had stolen three books of tickets from a drawer in the newspaper office. Poague and another friend of Bartlett's took the tickets to a drugstore, filled them out, and then put them in the ballot box.[14]

The next afternoon, Aull stopped by Bartlett's school and told her what had occurred. He gave her a few days to decide whether she wanted to abandon her claim to the piano or allow the court to determine the recipient. Soon after Aull's visit, Bartlett sent word that the piano was to be delivered to her. Aull refused this request, of course, as well as a similar demand by her friends.[15]

The controversy came to a head on Monday, January 17, when several of Bartlett's friends headed over to Rhodes Music Company, loaded the piano onto a wagon, and hauled it away. The piano was taken to the home of Bartlett's uncle, who lived four miles out of town. Aull immediately filed a writ of replevin with the court that afternoon, and the piano was confiscated the next day.[16] Now, his only course of action was to sue Bartlett for ownership of the instrument, although that meant waiting three months until the Barton County circuit court was in session.

After deliberating six or seven hours during the April trial, jurors voted 9 to 3 to award the piano to Aull. He had hoped that it could be handed over immediately to Nina Adams, but the outcome of the contest still had not been settled. Aull's attorneys announced that they would file a bill of equitable interplea so that Adams and Bartlett could present their evidence in court and allow a jury to determine at last the recipient of the piano.[17]

Aull displayed unusual restraint in withholding most of the facts of the caper until after the April trial, when he published a detailed history of the piano case. All along, he attempted to protect Bartlett's reputation, even calling her "a bright young woman of fine appearance, and unquestioned pluck and courage."[18] He refused, at least publicly, to acknowledge the fact that she may have encouraged her friends to stuff the ballot box or had at least been made aware of their actions. Aull afforded few others such treatment during his long stint as editor of the *Democrat.*

The piano was returned to the Rhodes Music Company, where it sat until December. On a change of venue, the Adams-Bartlett hearing was moved fifty miles north to Butler, Missouri. Bartlett's attorneys contended that the twelve-year-old Adams was ineligible to enter the contest in the first place because the *Democrat* had said it would award the piano to "the young woman" accumulating the most points. They also argued that Adams's friends had boosted her point total by purchasing numerous subscriptions themselves. After a three-day trial that was well attended, jurors deliberated only briefly before returning a unanimous decision for Adams.[19] The piano was delivered to the girl on New Year's Eve 1910, a year after the contest had closed.

FIVE HUNDRED DOLLARS IN GOLD

Undaunted by the shenanigans resulting from his piano contest, Aull waited but four months before launching another subscription drive. This time, though, he was careful to publish a detailed list of rules and regulations. The contest would run five months, with each new subscriber to the weekly *Democrat* receiving 1,100 votes in May, 1,075 votes in June, 1,050 votes in July, 1,025 votes in August, and 1,000 votes in September to award to the contestant of his or her choice. The new subscribers must live outside of Lamar and sign up to take the paper for an entire year. The contestant with the most votes would receive four hundred dollars in gold, the runner-up one hundred dollars in gold. The person who originally nominated the grand winner would receive twenty dollars in gold.

To prevent a recurrence of the piano contest fiasco, Aull stated that the ballot box would be kept locked, with the key safeguarded by "a disinterested third party." At the close of the contest, on September 30, 1911, the two leading contestants each would name a judge to count the votes. The two judges were to name a third judge, and the three-some would have final authority in awarding the five hundred dollars in gold.[20]

Primarily because of the piano contest, the circulation of the weekly *Democrat* had jumped from 1,000 in 1909 to 3,512 in 1911. The daily *Democrat*'s circulation had also tripled, from 300 in 1909 to 937 in 1911. The *Democrat*'s readership was more than twice that of the *Leader* (1,600 weekly and 400 daily) and the *Republican-Sentinel* (1,600 weekly). Still, Aull wasn't satisfied. In explaining the motivation behind the gold contest, he wrote, "But we want more. If there is anything in merit, the *Democrat* certainly shouldn't be satisfied with merely having the largest list of readers in the county. It should have the most by three times over, yes, four times. And that is why we institute this contest. New people are coming in and subscribing every day, but we must get hold of many at once. We want one more grand, vigorous boost."[21]

The *Leader* organized its own subscription contest, with prizes consisting of a trip to Niagara Falls, a diamond ring, a gold watch, and a scholarship to a business college. The contest was a washout, though. The *Leader* ultimately dropped its daily edition and reported a net loss of 750 subscribers in 1912.[22]

While not quite as successful as his piano contest, Aull's second subscription drive ended without any illegalities. Miss Alpha Isenhower claimed the four-hundred-dollar prize with 210,650 votes, while Mrs. M. S. Copeland won the one-hundred-dollar prize with 119,035 votes. The two finalists congratulated each other and sent letters to the *Democrat* thanking its readers for their support and Aull for originating the idea.[23]

Through the two contests, Aull boosted the *Democrat*'s combined weekly and daily circulation from 1,300 to nearly 5,000. His readership now surpassed that of White's *Emporia Gazette,* although Emporia's population exceeded Lamar's by nearly four times. But while the bulk of White's circulation came from the daily *Gazette,* Aull depended on the weekly *Democrat* for most of his readership. Although the piano and gold contests had induced many of his new subscribers, Aull recognized that the *Democrat*'s mounting reputation for publishing all the community's news was playing a significant role: "The *Democrat* has built up this subscription by printing the news as it happens, taking no note in reporting matters of public interest, of likes and dislikes and giving the people a paper from which they can actually get the news. In fact, if you want the actual news in Barton county, you've got to get it through the *Democrat*. It isn't published anywhere else."[24]

After the high-water mark of 4,995 in 1912, the *Democrat's* combined daily-weekly circulation hovered between 4,700 and 4,800 for the rest of the decade. It dipped to lows of 2,967 in 1926 and 2,805 in 1935, but by Aull's death in 1948 had climbed to 4,160.[25]

HARD TIMES

Fifteen years after he assumed control of the *Democrat,* Aull was still bemoaning the fact that three newspapers were attempting to scratch out a living in Lamar when the town, for all practical purposes, could support only one.[26] The *Democrat* supplemented its advertising and circulation revenues by printing wedding invitations, other announcements, stationery, and envelopes, but by 1918 had lost a considerable portion of its job printing business to print shops in neighboring cities. Rural newspapers everywhere were suffering because of the war, said Aull, who painted a dismal picture for the country editor:

> In the old days, if the proprietor of a country paper could make ten or twelve hundred dollars a year, above his office expenses, he got along very well. Now, he finds he would do better financially to chuck a job that pays him any such figure and go to work on a steam shovel, or in a munition factory. In former days there was plenty of reliable, pretty cheap help. Today, help in a print shop is scarce. The country paper is almost driven to buy an expensive machine, costing from twenty five hundred dollars up, and this is a great burden upon the average print shop. The small town merchants don't advertise like they did in years agone. Day by day, the country papers are quitting. You don't hear any more of ambitious local politicians starting a new paper. The ranks of country newspapers, during the next five years, will be recruited by practically no births, and decimated by many deaths.[27]

Shortly after the end of World War I, the escalating cost of newsprint forced Aull to raise the cost of his weekly edition from a dollar to a dollar and a half a year. He announced that "long winded explanations or apologies" would not be forthcoming, since the *Democrat* simply could no longer stay afloat at the dollar rate.[28]

Barton County farmers, who had increased production during the war to meet the demand in Europe, continued to earn higher prices for their corn, wheat, oats, and other crops after the armistice. Cattle and hog farmers also enjoyed the postwar prosperity. But in 1921, when the Federal Reserve Bank decided to deflate the currency, the agricultural community felt the impact almost immediately. Prices for corn plunged to a third of the 1919 level; cotton, wheat, and hogs tumbled to half the 1919 figure, and cattle to almost half. Yet the prices of commodities that the farmers had to purchase did not deflate, further compounding their plight.[29] As a result, bankruptcy rates skyrocketed. Thousands of Corn Belt farmers had financed additional land and livestock, new machinery, and improvements to their homes through borrowed capital, and deflation made it nearly impossible to repay those loans.

As deflation eroded the advertising lineage in the *Democrat*, Aull's disposition also soured. When a Dr. J. R. Montgomery, new to Lamar, wrote a bad check to cover a twenty-one-dollar advertising debt, Aull suspected that he might skip town and saw to his arrest. Montgomery's wife pawned her diamond ring the next day, permitting the doctor to be released from jail. Two months later, Aull cautioned *Democrat* readers that running a newspaper was similar to "walking a tight rope." He wrote: "If the newspaper doesn't sell it[s] space, it's [a] loser, that's all there is to it. . . . For years past the cost of getting out a paper has increased. Even in these times, when it's so hard to get hold of money, the tendency is for these expenses to get higher rather than lower. A newspaper is hard to sell. You will find very few people, not in the business, who want to own a paper, and many of those who are in; only wish somebody would help them let go."[30]

With the downturn in the *Democrat*'s financial situation, Aull continued to look for ways to broaden the paper's appeal to both subscribers and potential advertisers. The *Democrat* started carrying the full Kansas City Livestock Market report in addition to the local market report in 1921. And in 1924, Aull introduced a "Come to Lamar to Trade" contest where nonresidents could vie for fifty dollars in gold every week for twelve weeks. For each dollar spent at a store that advertised in the *Democrat*, shoppers received a ticket worth one hundred points. Every Saturday, the five customers accumulating the most points that week split the fifty dollars. Aull hoped to pay for the six-hundred-dollar promotion by selling the tickets to the participating businesses for a penny apiece, but he brought in only $418.14. "Even though the scheme went through with an appreciable loss to the paper and we're most certainly not so darned rich, that we can ignore losses, the feeling inside the office, is that all in all it was a good thing," he wrote, adding that the *Democrat* was likely to conduct another such contest again.[31]

THE KU KLUX KLAN COMES TO TOWN

Still another threat to the *Democrat's* existence came from the national resurgence of the Ku Klux Klan in the 1920s. The secret society had established newspapers in some communities, siphoning away precious advertising dollars and taking control of city and county offices. Aull was determined that the Klan not gain a foothold in Lamar, as much for his own sake as that of the town's. He had heard rumors of several carloads of men wearing white masks meeting south of town, but no real indication that trouble was afoot came until one Sunday night in June 1922. The Rev. R. N. Jones, pastor of the local Methodist church, stepped to the pulpit and delivered a sermon extolling the virtues of the Klan. The minister closed by asking in prayer that the Klan receive the divine blessing.[32]

Two weeks later, Aull cautioned readers that "it doesn't take a very wise man to see that a Ku Klux Klan is being organized, in this old town." A crowd of about one thousand gathered on the courthouse lawn a few nights later to hear a long-winded Klan orator from Georgia state that the group wanted to keep the "[N]egro, the Jew, the Catholic, the foreigner" out of public office. Newspapers, he said, were not particularly fair in their coverage of the Klan. That statement proved to be prophetic the next day as Aull's story in the *Democrat* contained more opinion than fact. It said, in part: "We would say that a lot of those people, who came to hear the address, went away disappointed. It was an unusually able speech, understand, and nine tenths of the folks in the big crowd agreed with just about everything the speaker said. But three of his hearers, out of four were secretly asking themselves before they came to the meeting, What is he going to say, about the gathering, of the white sheeted figures, bearing the fiery torch? What of the skull and cross bones? How about the tar and feathers?"[33]

That attempt to establish a Klan organization in Lamar died out, but six months later the stewards of the Methodist church voted 7 to 5 to permit a Klansman to speak at a special meeting. The meeting was scheduled for Friday evening, February 2, 1923, and a notice was brought in to the *Democrat* office by a man named Otto Nohrenburg to run in the Tuesday, Wednesday, and Friday papers. The announcement appeared in Tuesday's edition, but the Wednesday *Democrat* stated that the meeting had been postponed indefinitely due to the weather. The next morning, Nohrenburg appeared at the newspaper office demanding to know who had turned in the cancellation notice. A quick investigation revealed that a man unsympathetic to the Klan cause had left it with the *Democrat* foreman. Aull found the man and demanded an explanation. "Well, I'm not going to deny it," he told the editor. "I took it down there. As to how I came to do it, and what is behind it, I'll tell, only on one condition. That is, it's not to be published." Aull told him in that case he didn't care to know, and the matter was dropped.[34] One might suspect that Aull himself was behind the announcement caper, but he played no tricks when it came to money. Nohrenburg had paid for three notices, and the *Democrat* was forced to issue a refund for the last two.

Aull continued to rail against the Ku Klux Klan, declaring that "most organizers cuss the newspapers. They have the right dog by the tail, too. The newspapers are one big reason that it will be very hard for an organization like the [K]lan to achieve anything like a permanent success." Therefore, the Klan started several papers of its own, including one just across the state line from Lamar in Mulberry, Kansas. Mulberry already had a newspaper, but as Aull explained to readers of the *Democrat,* the editor, M. F. Sears, "has not been much inclined to give the Kluckers a chance to put their side of the case before the community." The Klan paper, the *Independent,* was edited by the Rev. E. H. Givens, who declared that Roman Catholicism and the liquor element were its greatest enemies.[35]

Back in Lamar, the Klan again attempted to organize, this time sending invitations to a large number of men in and around Lamar to meet at the Opera House on Monday evening, December 10. Each married man was invited to bring his wife. "Just how this will succeed is not known," Aull wrote. "In spite of the ridiculous side, that the Klan presents to the public, in its ghostly regalia, its Wizards, Grand Dragons and Oogles, it appeals to sentiments that are very strong in the heart of many a native American." Aull could hardly contain his excitement a few days later after making a rare appearance at the Baptist church on a

Sunday evening to hear the Rev. L. C. Wolfe's farewell sermon. Just as the minister stood up to speak, a "ghost-like" sheeted figure entered the church, walked up to the pulpit, and handed him an envelope. The mysterious stranger proceeded to deliver a short speech in which he praised the minister and said that the Klan stood for the church and the home. The envelope, which contained twenty dollars, was an offering made in the name of the Ku Klux Klan, he said. With that, the "ghostly apparition" left the church. In his story in the *Democrat,* headlined "Wow! Wow!! Wow!!!" Aull warned: "Keep your eyes on your p's and q's. Watch your step. Go joy ridin' with your own wives and doncha by any mistake go ridin' with any other guy's wife. Walk straight and go early to bed. The Ku Klux Klan has come to town."[36]

The Opera House was filled to capacity for the membership meeting. Aull, who estimated the crowd at four hundred or more, noted that "four sheeted and hooded Klansmen stood at the door, taking up the tickets." The speaker, a preacher from Kansas, wore a long, white gown and a cape lined with red silk. A layman, Aull chortled, might have mistaken him for a Catholic priest. The speaker, during his two-and-a-half-hour address, alluded several times to "an unfriendly newspaperman being present, and what he might say."[37] The crowd remained attentive throughout, applauding heartily more than once.

Those present were given cards to fill out indicating their interest in joining the Klan. Apparently the response was discouraging, for the Klan concentrated its efforts on Liberal, in the western part of Barton County. The "pillow slip boys," as Aull called them, won the marshal's office there and one of three aldermen's seats in the April 1924 elections. An alarmed Aull wrote, "The vote the [K]lan candidates got, Tuesday, shows that the sheeted order is almost ready to take over the town."[38]

The Ku Klux Klan made one final attempt to add Lamar to its fold in the summer of 1924. Members from Liberal and Nevada, Missouri, along with the fifteen or so Klansmen in Lamar, donned their robes and hoods and paraded around the square. A burning cross was planted on the courthouse lawn, but someone kicked it over minutes later. The caravan of about fifty marched on to the Christian church and entered humming "Onward Christian Soldier," then asked the minister to lead them in prayer. This accomplished, the Klan's spokesman asked to make a brief address, during which he presented the minister with a twenty-five dollar offering.[39]

A few weeks later, another Klan delegation from Liberal arrived in Lamar to present a program on the courthouse lawn. As the speaker began to address the large crowd, someone threw a tear gas bomb not far from the bandstand where the sixteen Klansmen sat. Those in the area "soon found themselves almost blinded by a severe smarting of the eyes, that made the tears fairly gush," Aull reported.[40] That was the Ku Klux Klan's last hurrah in Lamar, and the organization was not to be heard from again.

ADVERTISING

Early in his career, Aull came to the conclusion that a newspaper's profit margin best reflected the true journalistic abilities of its publisher. Of the three main sources of revenue—advertising, subscriptions, and job printing—the latter two merely covered the everyday expenses of running a newspaper. Local and legal advertising permitted the country editor to turn a profit, albeit a small one. The number of competing papers in a town or county diminished any net gain, something Aull bemoaned in a 1906 speech before the Missouri Press Association: "The average county seat has as many newspapers as a poor man has children. Where there should be two, there are almost invariably three, often four, and sometimes five. Not a few of the proprietors, as a consequence of the hopeless number of their competitors, sit around patiently waiting for the paper of one of their contemporaries to die."[41]

The *Democrat*'s booming circulation helped to convince many local merchants that Aull's newspaper was the best means of reaching customers both in and outside of Lamar. Others had to be educated about how advertising could help stop the flow of business to Sears and Roebuck and other mail-order houses. Aull's approach consisted of studying a retailer who did not advertise and determining the type of advertising he needed. After preparing an appropriate ad, he would make his sales pitch in hope of picking up a long-term account. Potential advertisers had to be "cultivated," Aull believed:

> Drop around to see them. It will give life and interest to your paper, and it will put you up next to them. Don't bore them. Don't press one too hard at any one time, but when you have started after a man, keep maneuvering until you land him, if it takes you a year.

> Don't be surprised, if when you first adopt this system, you often get
> turned down. You are almost sure to get many negative answers. But
> remember that there are not many people who can finally stand
> against patient persistence, good humor and intelligent effort.[42]

Still, Aull was more likely to return with a story for the newspaper
than with an ad. Ultimately, he relied on the editorial side of the *Democrat* to sell the requisite lineage; he believed that a "live newspaper" bol-
stered subscriptions and attracted advertising. Therefore, he expended
most of his effort in search of the story that would titillate readers and
compel Lamar's business community to take note. According to Aull,
"A paper, so gotten up, that the merchant notices his family and his
neighbors are anxious to read it, and so conducted that he observes that
people have to pay for it when they get it, will finally impress him more
as a good advertising medium."[43]

Aull's greatest advertising coup was landing the account of T. W.
Harkless and Company, a dry goods and clothing store that was the
largest retail establishment in Barton County. "Toss" Harkless, one of
the county's leading Republicans, entrusted the bulk of his advertising
budget to the *Democrat* until he closed "Lamar's Great Store" in January 1929. An admirer of Chicago department store magnate Marshall
Field, Harkless's innovations included locating his office in the midst of
his emporium to oversee everything and installing the first public rest-
room for women in Lamar.[44]

Unlike William Allen White and other country editors, Aull did
not automatically reject the placement of display advertising on page
one. Occasionally, a Harkless ad filled the entire front page of the *Democrat,* or at least half the page. And to further indulge the "merchant
prince," as Aull called him, the *Democrat* accorded him numerous
pseudo-stories over the years—his frequent buying trips to Chicago,
new lines of clothing offered by the store, and even a guided "tour" of
the entire operation.[45]

According to Aull, Harkless was the first in Barton County to sense
the onset of the Great Depression. The "merchant prince" intended to
close out his store and retire a wealthy man, but at the last minute re-
neged and stayed in business. The decision was a costly one, as Harkless
was nearly penniless by the time the store finally closed in January 1929.
Aull, about to lose his biggest advertiser, tried to put the end of
"Lamar's Great Store" into perspective: "To us older denizens of Lamar

it seems like the passing of a dynasty, the close of a local historic chapter, the severing of the last great link that binds us to all older traditions
of Lamar. Now comes the last act. The stock is to be sacrificed until it is
gone. The princely and beloved Toss will then be there no more. There
will be more than regret when this occurs. There will be genuine
sorrow."[46]

Despite losing T. W. Harkless, the *Democrat* enjoyed a banner year
in 1929. Aull ordered a press with greater capacity and put the paper's
antiquated four-page Babcock Reliance press and Omaha folder up for
sale. The larger Goss Comet press was essential, because he planned to
convert the *Democrat*'s timeworn weekly edition to a twelve-page semi-
weekly. The semi-weekly made its debut on October 1, 1929, with an
announcement from Aull that subscribers to the weekly would receive
papers on Tuesday and Friday for the same cost. "The new paper is gotten out to take care of much matter it was thought might possibly be interesting to the readers, that had to be left out, with but one paper," he
wrote.[47]

Throughout most of his editorship Aull disdained special advertising
editions, believing they could ruin a newspaper:

> When you have finished your special edition, you find that you
> have been at no small expense, the folks out in the composing room
> are worked to death, the type and stones look like your shop had been
> visited by a band of Russian Nihilists, you have neglected every other
> department of the paper and the merchants all want to lie out awhile
> and economize until they make up for what they have paid you on the
> extra advertising. After you get out one of these editions, you often
> find yourself with the same unhappy prospect as faced the little boy,
> who ate the custard off his pie. There's nothing but the crust left.
> Then, this class of advertising yields a poor return to your patrons.
> One regular reader is worth more to them than five or six recipients of
> a chance sample copy.[48]

Still, there was plenty of money to be made from advertising editions.
Aull finally gave in and published a twelve-page "Ad Reading Issue" in
1927. The edition featured thirty-four ads and an Aull slogan (such as
"Hardly a Reader Not Interested In At Least One Ad in the Paper. Find
Yours!") bannered across the top of every page. Out-of-towners were
urged to drive in for the numerous Saturday specials at Lamar's retail establishments. And Aull gently reminded everyone that newspaper ad-

vertising was fundamental to a newspaper's existence rather than a nuisance to be disregarded.[49]

In the 1940s the *Democrat* began publishing special Thanksgiving and Christmas editions in which local merchants could send holiday greetings to the people of Lamar and Barton County. The businesses composed the messages themselves, which were scattered throughout the paper in a display format. The holiday editions were highly profitable to the *Democrat,* evidenced by the 1944 Christmas issue, which drew a record fifty-six messages.[50]

As the bustling trade center of Barton County, Lamar had enough businesses advertising regularly in the *Democrat* to enable the Aulls to live comfortably but not extravagantly. Three of the town's five grocery stores advertised heavily in the paper, as did the two motor companies, the two oil companies, the service stations and garages, the clothing and shoe stores, the variety stores, the hardware and furniture stores, the lumber companies, the wallpaper and paint stores, Southwestern Bell Telephone Company, and Konantz Music and Undertaking. The *Democrat* also ran auctioneers' notices, business cards from local professionals, ads from businesses in neighboring towns, and such national ads as Wrigley's Chewing Gum, Doan's Pills, and Snow King Baking Powder.

The *Democrat* produced sufficient revenue to support an office/circulation manager, a shop foreman, a Linotype operator, an assistant, and a printer's devil while still allowing Aull to pocket about eight thousand dollars annually by the 1940s. According to a *St. Louis Post-Dispatch* correspondent who visited the editor two years before his death, "His electrically powered flat-bed presses, two [L]inotype machines and modern addressograph are the envy of rival publishers throughout Barton County." Although he spent freely on equipment, Aull still could afford to pay the largest grocery bill in town, hire a maid, and send all three of his daughters to the University of Missouri, some two hundred miles away.[51]

"THE CASE OF A GOOD MAN ENTHRALLED BY LIQUOR"

Just as he published all the community's news, Aull also accepted all of its advertising. This created a conflict early in 1936, when a group of sixty-five prominent Barton Countians demanded that the *Democrat* ban any future mention of beer, whiskey, or other alcoholic drinks in its advertisements.[52]

When Prohibition ended on April 7, 1933, beer could be sold and consumed legally in Lamar for the first time in twenty-five years. About two dozen men gathered at a junction west of town that Friday afternoon to meet the truck loaded with cases of Country Club beer. Within twenty minutes, the six establishments in Lamar possessing beer permits were serving the lukewarm beverage to customers lined up against the short-order counters and around the tables. Some tried to see how many bottles they could drink as the afternoon turned into evening, but there were no reports of drunkenness. Aull noted that "the beer carries with it a mild glow, nothing more."[53]

But in the case of fifty-nine-year-old George Petgen, the beer drinking led to the imbibing of hard liquor and eventually alcoholism. When Petgen was placed in the county jail for his wife's protection in 1935, Aull duly described the tragic turn of events in a story headlined "The Case of a Good Man Enthralled by Liquor." That the *Democrat* carried occasional advertisements for Bondwood whiskey stirred the group of sixty-five citizens into action. They expressed their appreciation for Aull's "frank" article but demanded, through a signed petition, that he ban all ads for alcoholic beverages.[54]

Aull told the "teetotalers" that he, too, abstained from whiskey, tobacco, and even coffee and tea, but did not believe in imposing his beliefs on others. Nonetheless, he said he would carefully consider their request to disallow the advertising since his views were often wrong.[55] Not wanting to set a precedent by bowing to community pressure, Aull nevertheless did stop running liquor advertisements. But the decision wasn't a difficult one; the small Bondwood whiskey ads brought in little revenue. Rubbing alcohol was the only kind that would ever be advertised in his *Democrat*.

THE NEW MEDIA

As the nation slowly began to recover from the depression in 1932 and 1933, Aull detected yet another economic threat to the *Democrat* and newspapers in general. Radio was starting to siphon away a considerable chunk of national advertising; about $150 million went to the new medium in 1933. The film industry, which had pumped millions of dollars into newspaper advertising in the 1920s, was among the first to test the airwaves. Aull, in fact, wondered whether radio had given newspapers their "death wound."[56]

The scientific development of "television radio," as he called it, also made him uneasy. Television was ten to fifteen years away, he predicted in 1933, but its advent would debase both newspapers and society. No one would attend major league baseball games, even the World Series, because the action would be visible on radio screens without charge. The National Broadcasting Co., by selling ads to the likes of Bulova, Blue Ribbon Beer, and Maxwell House, would compensate the teams. Movie theaters would close, as would most of the churches. Religion would be dispensed in every home by television evangelists and their bands of choir singers. And newspapers, according to Aull, would never see another line of national advertising.[57]

Radio presented an immediate threat, however, and Aull felt power-less to stop it from becoming the dominant medium. In 1940 he wrote: "Will radio, in the course of a few more years, run the newspapers entirely out of the field? We can't help but think it will. For one reason, while the papers run a lot of silly stuff, even at that they can't get down to the level of the boys on the air for pure silly assaninity—so it looks like the air's bound to win."[58]

A CHANCE FOR STARDOM

Much to his surprise, Aull received an opportunity to join radio shortly after rebuking the new medium in the *Democrat*. John U. Reber, vice president in charge of radio for the J. Walter Thompson advertising agency, phoned one December night in 1940 to invite him on an all-expenses-paid trip to New York to collaborate on a radio program for the rural consumer. The witticisms and homespun flavor of the *Democrat* had caught Reber's interest, particularly the fictitious characters created by Aull who had entertained readers for thirty years.

Reber's brainstorm called for Aull to star on a radio program sponsored by "one of America's great corporations." The corporation's identity was never revealed, but it was not Westinghouse as Aull originally had been told. J. Walter Thompson hoped to find another personality in the mold of Bob Burns, a hillbilly comedian from Arkansas who starred with Bing Crosby on "The Kraft Music Hall" radio show.[59]

That John Reber contacted Aull directly demonstrated the ad agency's interest in the country editor. Reber, regarded as radio's "first and probably greatest entrepreneur," managed J. Walter Thompson's radio department, which did everything from creating the concepts to producing the shows. Reber, with a sharp eye for new talent, thought he could bring stardom to Aull as he had done for Rudy Vallee, Eddie Cantor, Edgar Bergen, George Burns, and Gracie Allen.[60]

Reber wanted Aull to come to New York within three or four days to discuss the venture, but with the Christmas rush nearing, Aull politely declined. Instead, he volunteered to go in January when the hubbub around the office had settled down. Reber was cool to this idea, however, and ended the conversation. Luanna Aull teased her husband "unmercifully" about passing up his chance for fame, and then the matter was forgotten.[61]

On the night of Thursday, February 6, 1941, the phone rang while Aull was eating a late dinner. He expected it to be his pressman saying the Goss Comet had broken down again. But it was Reber, two months after his initial call, offering the editor a second opportunity to come to New York. Aull said he could be there Monday. Reber wired him a few hundred dollars to cover expenses, and a TWA flight from Kansas City to New York was booked for Monday morning.[62]

Except for the time spent in Kentucky and Illinois as a boy, the sixty-eight-year-old Aull had never ventured east of St. Louis. His first trip on an airplane disappointed him, as he found the six-hour flight extremely dull. However, the plane's speed, 232 miles per hour, did impress him, as did the meal of roast duck, potatoes, dressing, and caramel pudding. He was met at the airport by two J. Walter Thompson employees and given a room at the Commodore Hotel, across the street from the Gray-bar Building where the ad agency was headquartered. Reber took Aull to dinner at an Italian cafe, where he followed the editor's lead by ordering liver. To Aull's astonishment, they were calling each other "Arthur" and "John" despite the fact that neither had touched a drop of alcohol.[63] They were joined by two other key players in J. Walter Thompson's radio department: Robert T. Colwell, a talent buyer, and Abbott K. Spencer, a producer-director.

Reber and Aull met again the next morning to discuss the details of the proposal. The program's script had been prepared, and a contract awaited Aull's signature. But for the money the ad agency would be paying him, Aull insisted on writing an epic for the program's sponsor rather than using the agency's colloquial script. With both men equally stubborn, the plan to make Aull a radio comedian was abandoned. He later reflected on their negotiations: "The original colloquial plan won. John said there were limitations about a company speaking so highly of itself as our epic would read. But from beginning to end, they were kindness itself, and they saw to it that the trip to New York did not cost us a cent."[64]

The talks concluded prematurely, Aull had three more days to spend in New York before his Saturday morning flight back to Missouri. He paid a surprise visit to his oldest daughter, Madeleine, who lived in New York with her husband, Carl Van Hafften, an insurance salesman. Madeleine took him to the Trinity Church Cemetery, where he paid homage to the graves of Alexander Hamilton, Robert Fulton, and several Revolutionary War heroes. Aull remarked that he felt as though he had been shaking hands with the Continental Army. Another stop was the Metropolitan Museum of Art. Madeleine described their experience in a column she wrote for the *Democrat* two weeks later:

> The first floor of the Metropolitan Museum was just his dish. Although I had been there many times I got more out of it this time, because of his wide knowledge of Egyptology, Roman and Greek history, etc. He made it all come alive as he measured the mummies, and called up much forgotten history to my mind. He didn't really care to go to the second floor where all the famous paintings are hung, but he thought mama would be disappointed if he didn't. When he went into the galleries he astounded everyone with this remark, "My understanding of painting is just a little less than that of a Hottentot." However he was familiar with the names of all the old masters and it was with great glee that he had planned to tell mama he had seen original Botticellis, Rembrandts, Raphaels, etc.[65]

SMALL-TOWN ROOTS

The trip to New York served to remind Aull that he was not willing to trade Muddy Creek for the Hudson River, the Lamar square for Times Square, or his yellow roadster for the subways, double-decker buses, and taxis that he noticed were so prevalent. Stardom beckoned, but he was content to live out the rest of his life in Barton County, Missouri, where his leadership and civic vision had been felt for more than forty years. J. Walter Thompson's offer was tempting, and Aull was flattered by all the attention, but in the end it came down to a sense of community. New York wanted him, but Lamar *needed* him. And like Ed Howe, William Allen White, and other country editors of his day, Aull was loyal to his small-town roots.

Never quite sure how the townspeople felt about him, though, Aull received an indirect indication during his absence. Luanna Aull attended a club meeting and was "deeply touched" by the barrage of kindhearted questions about his trip. In her "Woman's Column" in the *Democrat* she wrote: "Knowing how he loves Lamar and its people, and how all of their joys and sorrows are his, how we wished he could have heard their delight and pleasure that he was to have such a fine trip—just as if they were his own sisters and daughters. If these lovely cultured women are a cross section of the readers of the *Democrat,* his efforts in behalf of their general interest have not been in vain. We are so glad he will get their posies while living."[66]

6

COMMUNITY

BETTERMENT

His interest in community affairs was unbounded. He wheeled his paper in behind any worthwhile project. Sometimes it struck pretty hard at the purse strings in taxes or donations, but he gave generously of his time and money.

—*Luanna Aull, September 6, 1957*

Throughout Barton County in the 1890s, Arthur Aull's name was synonymous with politics. His black mane blowing in the wind, he could be found at any Democratic Party gathering waving his arms and shaking his fists. He once wrote: "I don't drink, I don't smoke, but I have a fatal weakness. I love to make speeches. That's why I bought this newspaper, so I can make speeches in print and nobody can stop me."[1] Although he had served as county surveyor before purchasing the *Lamar Democrat* in 1900, Aull considered office holding the worst occupation a man could choose. He wrote in 1904:

> It often unfits a man for business, and it nearly always fastens upon him a number of expensive habits. However lucky he may be, there comes a time when the office holder is out of a job. Then he is a human wreck tossing helplessly upon the waves of life. He has been assailed and maligned until people have no confidence in him. But worse than that they pass him up as a has been, and let him go. He can

no more turn his back upon politics and go back to work at some gainful occupation, than a ruined and broken down gambler can keep from haunting the card tables.[2]

Job security was paramount to Aull, who now had a wife and family to support and a bank loan to pay off. All political opportunities extended to him as editor of the primary Democratic party organ in Barton County were automatically rejected. But late in 1914, he was offered a political plum that he couldn't refuse: the appointment as postmaster of Lamar. The perquisite came courtesy of Democratic Congressman Perl Decker of southwest Missouri, whom Aull had backed in 1912 and again two years later. The term of the Republican postmaster was set to expire in 1915, and it was up to Decker to recommend a replacement to President Wilson. The job paid $2,100 a year and, more importantly, would allow Aull to continue serving as editor and publisher of the *Democrat*.[3]

Aull was the only Barton County newspaperman to be recommended for a post office that year. To his surprise, his fellow editors reacted to the appointment with kudos rather than the "poison" he expected. The *Liberal News* called him "perhaps the most quoted editorial writer in this part of the country."[4] The greatest compliment came from the *Greenfield Vedette* in neighboring Dade County. Of all the tributes bestowed upon Aull during his lifetime and after his death, this early one is among the most significant. The writer, Phil Griffith, assessed Aull's qualities:

> Editor Aull runs an unusual paper at Lamar. A brilliant writer, he passes the news out to the Democrat constituency exactly as it happens. Nothing is concealed, or suppressed, or overlooked; for fear, or favor, or hope of reward. If Congressman Decker should go to Lamar tomorrow morning and get drunk, and beat up the nightwatch, and get pinched and thrown into jail, and fined, and given hours to leave town, the afternoon edition of the Democrat would tell the story without omitted a single detail of interest, and the postoffice job, which hinges on Decker's endorsement, could go hang. It might be supposed that this kind of a publication in a town the size of Lamar would not only make its publisher so unpopular that he couldn't run a good sixth in a contest in which only six were entered, but that it would be the direct cause of several men's sized cases for personal assault in the police court each week; but it doesn't work that way at Lamar. Editor Aull hasn't been licked for a long, long time.[5]

Aull served as postmaster of Lamar from August 1915 to January 1924. His duties included establishing and arranging the rural routes, hiring rural mailmen, sorting the day's mail and placing it in the post office boxes, weighing parcel post packages, and determining ways to increase the post office's revenue. Prior to his appointment, receipts had never reached the ten-thousand-dollar mark in any single year. The post office passed that benchmark in 1916, Aull's first full year on the job. That qualified Lamar for city delivery, and Aull wasted no time in asking postal authorities for the service. A postal inspector spent two days in Lamar early in 1917 laying out routes for city carriers and collaborating with Aull on delivery schedules. The inspector asked that street signs be posted at every corner, and every house numbered. This done, Aull awaited formal notification from the Post Office that city delivery would commence in Lamar. Instead, he received a letter stating that the town's population wasn't dense enough for the service. He didn't pursue the matter any further. The downtown businesses had reminded him that door-to-door mail delivery was not in their best interests, as people would not need to come to the square on a daily basis.[6]

As postmaster, Aull was permitted to appoint an assistant. Several men sat for the examination, but the position went to George Ward, foreman in the *Democrat* office, out of loyalty. Ward was able to remain assistant postmaster until retiring in 1947 at the age of seventy. Aull also helped another old friend, Will Jones, the barber, by giving his son a job until his "unfortunate weakness" (drinking) caused his dismissal from the post office.[7]

Postal receipts continued to grow in Lamar, topping $16,500 by the time Aull left office. The increase in business had boosted his postal salary to $2,500 a year, and he hated to step down.[8] But the election of a Republican congressman in 1922 meant that when Aull's term expired on January 24, 1924, the appointment would go to a Republican.

A RUN FOR THE SCHOOL BOARD

Though he worked eleven-hour days, even on Sundays, Aull's appetite for greater civic involvement grew as he reached middle age. Believing "there should be marked and sweeping changes in the management and conduct of the Lamar public schools," he announced his intention to run for the school board in March 1917. His campaign platform had three main planks. The first was to end the board's practice of meeting privately in members' offices. Aull suggested the board meet at a public place and post the time, date, and agenda of its meetings beforehand. Second, he proposed that most homework be eliminated. "I am against the practice of requiring pupils to spend six hours over their books in school, and then insisting they spend from three to four hours more in study at home," he stated. Third, he wanted to eliminate all nepotism by the board in hiring teachers or contracting services. Aull also called on the superintendent of schools to take a more active role in disciplining teachers who defied the board's authority.[9]

Four days later, an overflow crowd packed the circuit courtroom to hear the president of the school board address Aull's criticisms. He spent twenty-five minutes refuting every one of the editor's points, declaring that the Lamar high school was one of the best in the state and that nothing could be done with an insubordinate teacher during the term of her contract. As for the excessive homework, he said state officials prescribed the amount. When the school board president finished, the crowd chanted "Aull, Aull," who simply called for nominations to the board. Aull and another man were elected by acclamation, but this didn't quiet the editor's followers. Again they called for the editor of the *Democrat* to speak. He finally stood up and announced that his suggestions for the operation of the school board had struck a nerve. Men would shout "I'm with you" from wagons, he said, as they passed him on the street. Aull admitted that he was no Moses, just an ordinary citizen who had to send his children to the Lamar schools.[10]

Near the end of his three-year term, Aull highlighted the school board's accomplishments. The board had unanimously passed a resolution that no teacher or other employee of the district should be related to any member of the board by blood or marriage. Relations between the board and the community had improved, he said, and now every citizen felt comfortable enough to bring any criticism before the board. And, perhaps most importantly, the district's teachers had reduced the amount of homework. Aull also noted that he had missed but a single board meeting, called at noon one day to discuss a special situation.[11]

Though he did not actively seek a second term on the school board, Aull left the door open for his renomination. "I have asked no man to vote for me," he stated in the *Democrat*, "and it is not my present intention to do so. I feel that with a fair turnout at the meeting, Friday evening, if the people generally approve my course on the board, they will probably elect me. If they disapprove, they will not."[12]

Lamar school board members were selected at a caucus, a mass gathering held the first Friday evening in April in the circuit courtroom. A Democrat and a Republican were elected every year to serve three-year terms. As president of the board, Aull called the 1920 meeting to order, then relinquished control when it became apparent that he wasn't going to be elected by acclamation this time. Will Earp and Mel Gelwicks were also named as candidates for the Democratic position; a lone Republican was named for the other spot. After the ballots were counted, it was announced that Aull had received fifty-three votes, Earp forty-six, and Gelwicks twenty-three. Because Aull had not received a majority, Gelwicks dropped out and the crowd voted again. This time Aull received sixty-seven votes to Earp's sixty.[13]

The issue was far from over, though. On Monday night a group of Earp backers charged the Aull camp with "illegal balloting" by allowing Luanna Aull and several other women to vote at the caucus. "It is not yet legal for women to vote in Lamar," they declared. Indeed, it would be another four months before women would win the right to vote in the United States. Aull's supporters, while not denying the charge, countered that some of Earp's friends had voted more than once. Earp was placed on the ballot again, this time as an Independent candidate, with the outcome to be settled in the next day's school levy election. That the school board had called a levy election gave Earp's backers added ammunition. Though he outwardly claimed to support the twenty-five-cent levy increase, his "Independent Nominating Committee" believed that an "imprudent management of funds" under Aull's leadership had brought about its necessity.[14]

Aull, initially ambivalent to a second term on the board, now felt that his pride and reputation were at stake. Will Earp, a first cousin to the legendary Wyatt Earp, was a formidable adversary; his well-oiled political machine would have made Tom Pendergast proud. The Earp gang controlled Lamar's Fourth Ward, located in the firehouse, and positioned workers at the town's three other wards. Much to Aull's chagrin, the Earps spent election day hauling men he didn't recognize to the Fourth Ward and arm twisting those he did know at the other polling places. A fight broke out at the Fourth Ward between George Earp, Will's younger brother, and an Aull supporter who showed either remarkable courage or stupidity in claiming that it would be a disgrace to elect Earp.[15]

Unable to concentrate much on his writing, Aull spent what he called the longest day of his life walking around town between the four wards. He later remarked that he wished he'd worn a pedometer to measure the mileage. He felt unusually strange; he had covered plenty of elections before, but this was the first time his "own bacon was in the fire." Aull all but conceded defeat when the *Democrat* went to press that afternoon, calling himself the "prospective corpse." He had heard from a friend that of the fifty-six votes cast thus far at the Fourth Ward, fifty belonged to Earp. "It was like a man standing off watching, his own funeral, under the deft management of a corps of crack undertakers," he noted.[16]

But that evening, with all the votes counted, Aull was stunned. He had defeated Earp 250 to 231, although he lost the Fourth Ward by 58 votes. There was a great temptation to crow, but that was not Aull's style. Instead, he simply thanked those who made his victory possible and announced that the episode had taught him an important journalistic lesson:

> If it hadn't been for the interest a lot of my friends and supporters took in the matter, I would have been snowed under too deep to dig out. They couldn't have taken more interest, if they had been in my place. A man who runs a newspaper hasn't much business in running, even for school director. It's too hard for him to keep an impartial view of things, and tends to establish a bias, that greatly impairs his service to his readers.
>
> Since the little school episode is over, I will try to fade out of the local limelight, get back, into the wings of the stage, where a humble chronicler of events always belongs, and give you something in the third person.[17]

Aull's feud with the Earp clan wasn't over, however. A year later, in 1921, he took the curious step of publicly supporting a Republican candidate for mayor over John Earp, Will's brother. The Republican, Paul Holmes, was a relative newcomer to Lamar who Aull believed presented a breath of fresh air in contrast to the Earp political machine. John Earp, one of the wealthiest men in town, had amassed a considerable fortune from jewelry and trucking businesses. As chairman of the Barton County Democratic Committee in 1896, he had played a key role in electing every man—including Aull—on the party ticket to office that year.[18] Earp was elected mayor of Lamar the following year, but lost his bid for reelection in 1899 when Aull helped to support the Republican nominee.

Earp never forgave Aull for his disloyalty, and the two maintained a strong dislike for each other over the next two decades. While Aull normally backed all Democrats for local and county office, he occasionally felt that a member of the other political party was better suited for the job. In Paul Holmes, president of the chamber of commerce, Aull thought Lamar had a "fine, clean, pleasing young man, and town builder" who had a "canny and sensible way of doing things, to get the very best he can for the town." To help Holmes's prospects, Aull published a list of Republican accusations against Earp, and in an unusual breach of his normal policy, failed to give the Democratic mayoral candidate the opportunity to respond. "If it hadn't been that we felt John would get sorer than ever, we'd have offered to run everything he wanted to say, along this line, in the paper," he explained. "But we figured John wouldn't appreciate any conversation from us, just then, so we kept still." But Aull had to find out firsthand what a mistake he had made. Earp found the editor that evening at the West Side Bakery and publicly chastised him, promising to seek revenge.[19]

The next day, Earp printed a campaign bulletin that attacked Aull for deserting the city's Democratic Party and boosting Holmes. A second bulletin further vilified the newspaperman: "It is high time for the Democrats to wake up to the true character of the Lamar Democrat. The wolf in sheep's clothing of the old fable had nothing on this wrongly captioned purveyor of Republican propaganda." Aull pointed out that Earp's publications mentioned nothing of his plans for the community, instead focusing entirely on his hatred of the *Democrat* editor. "Why pay all of the attention to Arthur Aull," he asked. "He has only one little measly vote, and it makes very little difference how he casts it."[20]

The day before the election, Aull took one last jab at Earp in the *Democrat:* "With all of his good qualities—and he has many good ones—you will see that John can't rise above the personal selfish way of looking even at public things. He wants to do things to get even." As it turned out, Aull likely cost the young Republican Holmes the mayoralty. Holmes lost by a mere forty-eight votes as many of the fence-straddling Democrats thought the election presented an opportunity to repudiate Aull's influence. "It might be that it had been better, if the writer, not wanting to see Mr. Earp mayor, and really thinking he would be a bad man for the town, should have lined up, and voted for him, and said nothing rather than to have come out and told what he thought about it," Aull noted.[21]

A CHAMBER OF COMMERCE FOR LAMAR

While serving on the school board, Aull helped to organize a chamber of commerce in Lamar. Fearful that the local Broom Factory would move to the neighboring city of Carthage, whose own chamber was wooing Lamar's largest employer, a group of twenty-six men each put up ten dollars in October 1919 to start an organization in Lamar. Aull, selected as one of the chamber's seven directors, also helped draft a set of by-laws. Citing a conflict of interest, he declined an appointment to the chamber's publicity committee. Instead, he was named chairman of the agriculture committee.[22]

The chamber wasted little time in establishing a permanent headquarters on the second floor of the new Hill Building, on the northeast corner of the square. To celebrate the occasion, the directors voted to serve a dollar-a-plate dinner. Aull, whose fondness for a good meal was known throughout Lamar, objected to their choice of food: "There are some things too much for pore weak human nature to bear. One of them is for the C of C, we have all made so much fuss about, to celebrate its housewarming, on a plate of thin lukewarm soup, with two or three lonesome, debilitated oysters, floating around on top." Another director suggested that the meal consist of wild game, and so it did. Ninety people gorged themselves on duck and quail furnished by a group of hunters and sportsmen who belonged to the chamber.[23]

The chamber's next order of business was to offer a ten-dollar award to the person submitting the winning slogan for the city of Lamar. The directors hoped to find something that reflected their goal of persuading voters to approve a bond issue that would improve the roads of Barton County. Of the 116 entries, they selected "Sell your hammer and buy a horn."[24] Aull bannered the slogan across the front page of the December 25, 1919, edition of the *Democrat* and offered a complimentary subscription to all county voters who sent their name and address to the chamber secretary.

The chamber voted unanimously to support "Good Roads and Road Bonds" and raise half of the thousand dollars needed for campaign expenses in Lamar. But a few days later, Aull sampled a large group of farmers gathered on the town square and found little support for the bond issue. "One of the things the boys harp on is the taxes," he reported. "They've already doubled. They don't want any more." Shortly after, the bond election was called off and the chamber of commerce set its sights on paving the square and building five miles of cement sidewalks.[25]

Aull considered his part in paving Lamar's massive square his greatest civic accomplishment. The four streets around the square were each one hundred feet wide and four hundred feet long, and to pave them would require some fifteen thousand square yards of cement. Property owners would share the considerable expense along with the county, and many immediately objected. But the current situation was unacceptable to Aull and other members of the chamber of commerce. On windy days, he observed that the dust and gravel from the streets "beat in the faces of pedestrians like sleet, depositing a layer of gravel on the sidewalks and sifting into the stores, every time a door was opened, doing no little damage to certain kinds of stock."[26]

Aull went around the square trying to talk business owners into paving the square from curb to curb rather than just putting a single strip down the middle, an idea which was gaining support. "He and the more progressive merchants felt that this was only half doing the job," his wife recalled years after his death. "He was never a believer in a half loaf." Aull reminded everyone that nearby Greenfield had paved its entire public square, although he admitted that its streets were narrower and its building frontage much less.[27]

The Lamar city council voted unanimously to pave all of the square in May 1926, six years after the chamber of commerce initially recommended such an undertaking. Still, there was one more obstacle to overcome. Sixteen property owners, including John Earp, Aull's old nemesis, signed a petition stating their opposition and presented it to the city clerk. The council met again and passed a resolution to proceed as planned since the signers of the remonstrance did not constitute a majority of property owners along the square. When it came time to open the bids a month later, an overflow crowd packed city hall and spilled out onto the sidewalk. The council moved the meeting to the chamber headquarters and awarded the contract to the Independent

Construction Company of Pittsburg, Kansas, which had submitted the low bid of $34,300.[28]

The job was scheduled to be completed in forty days, by the end of September, but heavy rains delayed the project's completion until December. The four sides of the square were closed completely for two months, causing merchants to lose considerable business. Finally, on a Saturday morning, the city's new fire engine sprayed the cement clean, and, fittingly, the street in front of the *Democrat* office was opened first. The editor paused to watch the occasion through the window, then stepped outside to join in the celebration: "When the north side was finally opened to traffic, about nine o'clock, the whole expanse on the four sides of the square was as clean as a newly scrubbed floor. It wasn't long until the cars were parked everywhere in the old convenient way. Folks found the paving mighty fine. No more jolting as they drove about the square. A nice cement pavement for the women folks to step out upon, wherever the car was parked."[29]

Two years later, after the square received a second "white way" (a brilliantly lighted section), Aull observed that it was becoming "one of the show places in this part of the country." He noted: "Its broad paved streets, the large green courthouse lawn, margined by the green nicely clipped privet hedge that is protected by the little fence with the red posts, all unite to please the eye."[30]

LAKE CEMETERY ASSOCIATION

Aull received little acclaim for his work on behalf of the Lake Cemetery Association in Lamar, but he helped establish a sound financial base for the cemetery during his twenty-five years as association president. Incorporated in 1880, the cemetery was to be governed by six trustees meeting annually. But forty years later, when the chamber of commerce initiated an investigation, the association's affairs were in disarray. The trustees had failed to meet for a number of years, no financial report had been filed for some time, and records of burials and plot ownership were sketchy at best. Management of the cemetery had been taken over by Hoyt Humphrey, an undertaker who was one of the six original trustees. Humphrey's critics charged that he had pocketed the money off the sales of the lots, sold two acres off the north side of the cemetery to a church without authorization, and used his control of the associa-tion to drive two competing morticians out of business.[31]

Under pressure from the Barton County prosecuting attorney to straighten out the mess, the chamber decided that any citizen could join the Lake Cemetery Association by filing a membership application, pay-ing a dollar, and receiving a two-thirds vote of the group. The entire membership would elect two new cemetery directors every year to re-place those whose terms had expired. The chamber recruited sixty-one new members for the association, and twenty-five of them gathered on a Tuesday night early in January 1921 to be voted in and then march over to Humphrey's store, where they would participate in the election of the two new directors. But then word was received that seventeen of the sixty-one potential new members had been rejected by the old directors. Aull was among the forty-four accepted members, who immediately voted that no one would attend the meeting that night at Humphrey's store.[32]

Cooler heads prevailed on both sides, and at a meeting six days later at Humphrey's, four of the existing six cemetery directors were replaced. Aull, acceptable to both factions, was elected. Shortly after, the directors named him president, a position he held until he stepped down in 1947. The new directors wasted little time in devising a plan to get the Lake Cemetery Association back on its financial feet. The cemetery pos-sessed 114 choice lots on its south side, which would be sold for three hundred dollars apiece. Two hundred dollars from each sale would be placed in an endowment fund, which in twenty years or so would amount to sixty thousand dollars. The interest on the sixty thousand would provide for the upkeep and maintenance of the cemetery indefi-nitely.[33]

In addition to the paving of the square, projects Aull supported in-cluded municipal ownership of a water and electric plant, a new county jail, an airport, and a modern hospital. He didn't live to see the comple-tion of the Barton County Memorial Hospital, but a 1945 editorial helped stir up enthusiasm: "A hospital for Barton County would be a tremendous advantage. There are many angles from which it can be considered. It would be a great thing if the sick in the county did not have to be hauled to Kansas City, to Springfield, to Joplin, to Carthage, to Pittsburg. It would also be of great advantage in getting good doctors to locate and remain in Lamar. Doctors with no hospital near at hand bear a great burden and labor under a great disadvantage. Naturally they prefer as a rule to locate elsewhere when this burden becomes too great."[34]

Before ground could be broken, though, the county first had to approve a tax levy. The plan was opposed initially by several residents of Liberal, in the western part of Barton County, and Golden City, in the eastern part of the county. The two towns' perennial rivalry with Lamar threatened to doom the project, but it passed by a 3,742 to 283 landslide in 1946.[35]

Aull also worked tirelessly to bring industry to Lamar. While the town's natural charms appealed to many visitors, the shortage of jobs meant they didn't stay for long. Outside of two broom manufacturers and a wire factory, Lamar offered little in the way of industry. "Factories!" he cried in 1929. "We pine for 'em, we're crazy for 'em, we dream about 'em. But we've never been able to get a factory to move here."[36] Aull suggested hiring an industrial consultant to advise the town as to what branch plants it might attract, making more of a systematic effort to bring in industry, and keeping an eye open for any small enterprise it could initiate locally.

BARTON COUNTY RELIEF COMMITTEE

When the Depression set back all plans for industrial development in Lamar, Aull turned his attention to the Barton County Relief Committee, charged by the Missouri Relief and Construction Commission with relieving the stress and destitution caused by unemployment. He had been appointed to the Barton County committee by Wallace Crossley, state relief administrator and a fellow newspaperman. Much of Crossley's work in 1933 and 1934 involved securing federal funds from several of President Roosevelt's New Deal agencies. Consequently, this meant the county committees would be subject to federal intervention, or the "traveling brain trusters" as Aull called them.[37]

An incident early in 1935 triggered his resignation from the Barton County Relief Committee. A "brain truster" visited Lamar to oversee the distribution of surplus food, which came off without incident. The agent, according to Aull, filed a report stating that an unruly crowd had gathered at the location, police were called in, and a wooden barricade was hurriedly constructed to secure the building. Aull mailed his resig-

nation to Crossley and urged other members of the local relief committee to do the same. He explained to readers of the *Democrat:* "[We] cut
about as much ice as a vermiform appendix. The brain trusters who
travel around over the state are running things in defiance of the local
committees." So controversial was Aull's resignation that the *New York
Times* even picked up the story on February 22.[38]

Aull maintained that although the "high priced messers" had claimed
otherwise, he still supported Roosevelt's New Deal. "No, we're for the
president," he wrote. "If he had time really to know about them, he'd
give them the boot. They're the people who're doing the President the
dirt, and they're doing it plenty." Crossley, the state relief administrator, refused to accept Aull's resignation and urged the editor to remain
on the committee.[39] Aull agreed to stay, but little else is known about
his later involvement.

7

F A M I L Y   M A N

Arthur had the very happy faculty of leaving his business cares behind him when he came home. He hurried in at evening with a merry greeting which was a signal for the family to gather around, with the children eager to tell him all of the happenings of the day. If they chanced to see him coming, they raced to meet him and had the big news, if any, all told before he got in the house. I never got to tell him any news after Madeleine learned to talk. When I would begin, a wise smile would cross his face and everyone began to laugh.

—*Luanna Aull, September 6, 1957*

The *Lamar Democrat* wasn't a mom-and-pop operation like many of the country papers of the early twentieth century. Luanna Aull seldom stepped foot in the *Democrat* office in the forty-eight years her husband edited the paper. "Sally," as he called her, preferred to remain at home raising the couple's three daughters and attending to the many relatives who lived with them. She believed that for a marriage to be successful, the husband must "work honestly and faithfully at his job" and the wife must "live within his income and keep a neat and comfortable home."[1] Her devotion to the family and her ability to run a household single-handedly permitted Aull to work the long hours at the *Democrat* and do the jobs of two or three men.

Luanna also spent a considerable amount of time cooking. Aull was slender when she married him; at a Missouri Press Association meeting in St. Louis, he was introduced as having the looks of Adonis and the brains of Socrates. But the five-foot-ten-inch Aull had a huge appetite, and his weight swelled to two hundred pounds over the next decade. Luanna once remarked that she had "snapped forty trainloads of green beans for that man."[2]

Fatherhood appealed to Aull, whose own childhood had been marred by the death of his mother and the remarriage of his father to a woman who showed him little affection. He lavished as much attention as possible on Madeleine, the Aulls' only child for nearly seven years. Luanna fondly recalled his insistence that she ride in the local Democratic Party's flambeau parade shortly before the elections of November 6, 1900. The midnight parade featured torch-bearing marchers, bands, donkeys, and three-year-old Madeleine dressed in a blue velvet coat and bonnet to match. It was her first taste of politics and the beginning of her lifelong interest.[3]

In addition to Mamma Sally, Aull had a nickname for every member of the family. Madeleine was "Honkie," perhaps because she blew her nose so loudly as a child. In any event, she kept the moniker the rest of her life. Daughter Genevieve, born to the couple on September 30, 1903, was "Keeser." And daughter Betty, who arrived on January 14, 1908, was "Betty Bean" or simply "Betts." As for Aull, "Yours Truly" sufficed the few times he mentioned himself in the *Democrat*.

Betty's birth received little fanfare in the *Democrat*. Unable to hide his disappointment at the sex of the new baby, Aull placed the announcement at the bottom of page four void of her name or any other vital statistics:

> Well, we suppose it's rather up to us to say something. An event has just transpired down at our house—not entirely unexpected. There has been a complaint upon the part of our honored president to the effect that such events are not happening in this country with sufficient frequency. Yet, we have heard no complaints upon that score upon the part of the women, and not so very many upon the part of the men. It might be pertinent to observe, before we get any further, that despite our long practice in writing up the affairs of this character, our progress thus far in telling about this particular event seems pretty disappointing. So we'll drop all of this trying to siddle up to the question gradually and say it's a girl, another girl, if you please. There isn't

very much to say about her, either, so far as we can see. Her mother says she's pretty, but to be real frank, we'll have to admit that she looks just about like all of the other girls of her age we have ever seen. We hope she may inherit her mother's virtues and at least none of her daddy's faults. Really, we believe we have now said about all that the occasion would seem to require, and, like as any way, even considerably more.[4]

Years later, when someone sympathized with Aull for not having a son, he replied that his daughters had served him well. Growing up, they provided the respite he so sorely needed after his eleven-hour days at the *Democrat*. After leaving the office, the children had his undivided attention. If Luanna didn't have the evening meal ready, he would pick up Betty and recite fairy tale rhymes as they paced the floor.[5]

Dinner at the Aull household was always a drawn-out affair, with the conversation focusing on current and world affairs and the girls relating their own adventures at school. The family then would move on to the living room, usually leaving the dishes for later. While Luanna sewed in her rocking chair, Arthur read poems, part of a novel, or a historical piece to the children, who had no set bedtime. Mamma Sally cherished those quiet evenings at home, long before radio and television would change family relationships forever. She later reminisced in her women's column: "When [our children] got sleepy they slipped off to bed or went to sleep on the big davenport. No one worried about that. We just took them up when we went. They hardly knew when we put them to bed. This will all seem crazy to the modern minded mother, but we had no begging to [stay] up and they gathered a lot of information they might have missed. They were always considered well informed youngsters in school and even in college."[6]

As a boy, Aull had developed the habit of reading far into the night. He normally read aloud, in a rapid and rhythmic cadence. He could choose from hundreds of books; the extensive library he assembled in his home boasted the works of all the great historians and poets. After the girls had gone to bed, he and Luanna would retire to their bedroom where they often read poetry to one another until 1 or 2 A.M. Sir Walter Scott was his favorite poet, but he also loved Thomas Moore. He was able to memorize many poems and often entertained Luanna by reciting the classics as they drove about the countryside.[7]

Early in their married life, the Aulls belonged to the Lamar Shake-speare Club, which presented a play every month at the home of a member. Everyone in the club owned a copy of *The Complete Works of William Shakespeare* and was assigned a role to learn for the next meet-ing. Madeleine, about eight years old at the time, insisted on watching the plays presented in the Aull home. She became enamored with the character of Portia, the heroine in *The Merchant of Venice,* and seriously considered changing her name to Portia.[8]

Aull didn't limit his acting to the Shakespeare Club. He portrayed the role of Boaz in the play *Ruth* presented by the 20th Century Club in Lamar, and either Julius Caesar or Marcus Aurelius during a talent show at the Lamar Opera House. Located on the south side of the square, the Opera House was at one time the center of all cultural activity for the town and surrounding area, according to Lamar historian Reba Young. Musical comedies, minstrels, melodramas, and Shakespearean troupes all made their way to its stage during the early 1900s. After the comedy *Irish Pawn Brokers* played the Opera House to glowing reviews, Aull wrote that "the management is getting us no small number of really first-class attractions for a town much larger than Lamar and our people should show their appreciation by their patronage."[9]

Aside from an occasional fishing trip, the Aulls never took any vaca-tions due to his insistence that the *Democrat* put out six issues a week, plus a weekly edition. He did build a camp cabin once on Muddy Creek east of the town, and the family spent many pleasant hours there. The editor even worked on Sundays, while Luanna and the girls were at the Presbyterian Church. He was an agnostic, but insisted that his children attend Sunday school.[10] Aull didn't drink or smoke, although he had plenty of other vices. He loved to eat, he was hot-tempered, and he was generally regarded as the champion cusser of Barton County.

Despite those faults, Aull was a great benefactor of the impoverished. His daughter, Betty, remembers him giving a hundred dollars to a young Presbyterian minister who was found hitchhiking out of town after the church abruptly discharged him. "He was a very modest man," she said. "Mr. Griffin, who had the biggest grocery store here, said you wouldn't believe the amount of groceries that Dad had sent out. When-ever he heard of a hungry family, he sent out good food, and lots of food. But he wouldn't allow them to tell who sent it." On two occasions, Aull did publicize his good deeds in the *Democrat.* He gave a panhandler a half dollar he had been saving for a Christmas haircut, and he posted bond for a poultryman arrested for possession of two bottles of corn liquor.[11]

His family benefited from his generosity as well. The Aull girls loved oranges and ate them by the sackful. When Luanna mentioned one morning that she couldn't buy the sacks fast enough to satisfy their demands, Aull had a crate of big, juicy oranges wrapped in tissue paper delivered to the house. "I'm going to fill those kids up on oranges," he said. The crate lasted only three days.[12]

Aull was a modest man. The subject of numerous feature articles toward the end of his career, he was mailed complimentary copies by the publications. He read them, of course, but they were immediately thrown in the trash. The *Democrat*'s office manager, Nell Casement, dug them out later and placed them and letters of admiration in a scrapbook she had started. And at dinner time, Aull never made any mention of his notoriety.[13]

Casement, who came to work for Aull in 1925, was a fixture in the *Democrat* office for the next forty-four years. Working at the front desk, handling the circulation, and managing the paper carriers, the former elementary school teacher shielded the "Boss" from many of the mundane tasks of running a newspaper. And as it did for Aull, the *Democrat* became her life and love.[14] The paper paid her the following tribute on the thirtieth anniversary of her employment:

> Very few days has she failed during these many years to greet customers with a smile and a saucy quip if the occasion demanded: like the time a customer pretended he was changing his subscription to a competitive paper. She never blinked an eye and let him go out as a lost subscriber. When he returned and admitted it was a hoax, she said "Well, I had a good notion to take you across my checkered apron!" She soothes the irate advertiser when his copy comes up with a mistake, and lectures the guilty boys in the composing room. If a boy fails to show up for delivery, the subscribers never miss their papers. She calls a taxi and delivers them herself. If the mailing list has to make a deadline at the post office she sees that the papers catch the mail. The editor and management can leave when their hard day is over, knowing Nell will see that the paper gets out. She loves boys and her little band of carriers are all strong for her. She lectures them but has infinite patience. Many of these boys are successful men now. Not a one

ever comes back to the home town but he makes a bee-line to the Democrat to see Nell.[15]

AULL BUYS A HOUSE

Preferring to invest any surplus money in new equipment for the
Democrat, Aull put off buying a house until 1920. The family moved
from rental home to rental home, starting with one next to the
Methodist parsonage when they moved to Lamar in 1900. The eight-
room, two-story house Aull purchased for thirty-six hundred dollars at
400 West Eleventh Street was only a four-block walk to the *Democrat.*
He later bought the adjoining lot north of the house for five hundred
dollars to make sure no one else would buy it and cut down the stately
elm that shaded the yard. The Aull home, always warm and flooded
with light, was at times overrun with the girls' acquaintances dancing to
the Victrola and wearing out the carpet. Parties and pancake suppers
were also held there regularly.[16]

The four-bedroom house, which boasted two front doors, a long
porch, and several nooks and crannies, was spacious enough to accom-
modate the many relatives who lived with them over the years. Aull's father had moved in with the family after the death of his second wife in
1910 and remained with them until his own death twenty years later.
Although they had relocated to Iowa, Luanna's father and stepmother
spent several months with them every year to escape the harsh northern
winters. And Flossie Turnbull, Luanna's sister, lived with the Aulls for
several years while she ran the front office of the *Democrat.*

So many other friends and relatives stopped by the Aull house that
Luanna sometimes felt overwhelmed by her household duties. When
any of her six sisters came to visit, they naturally assisted her in the
kitchen and in cleaning up afterward. Aull's cousins, though, would remain in the living room or on the porch while she prepared the meal
and washed the dishes. He confided to readers of the *Democrat* that this
made her "tired and cross." Furthermore, he said, she didn't have "the
nerve to tell the visitors how she feels, so she takes it out on pore ole A.
Mrs. A doesn't belong to the domestic workers union, but when she
has to cook and clean up for a bunch of her husband's folks, she feels
and acts a good deal like a hired girl does when she thinks the family is

having too much company." William Aull, or "Grandpa" as everyone called him, presented no burden to the Aulls the twenty years he lived with them. Much of his time was spent planting and tending a garden that encompassed the entire back yard. "He was a real farmer and loved the soil," Luanna recalled many years after his death at the age of eighty-two. "And he and Arthur seemed very happy together." William Aull loved the open spaces and liked to take long walks with his son in the woods that grew along Muddy Creek.[17]

Unexpected guests were also quite common at the Aull home. So many stayed for dinner that Luanna always kept biscuits on hand as a complement to any other food she might serve. Everyone liked hot biscuits with butter and jam, she figured. When syndicated columnist Ted Cook arrived in Lamar unannounced one afternoon, Luanna was quickly summoned from a card party: Cook and his wife would be coming for dinner and would spend the night at the Aull residence. Most hostesses would have panicked at such short notice, but not the editor's wife. Twenty years later, she relived the incident: "We were just leaving so we soon hurried home, found a fruit salad in the ice box and some steak. We set the table, made some biscuits and fried the steak. With some pickles we had a dinner they really enjoyed. However Ted and Arthur were so busy looking each other over and sizing each other up and exchanging quips and jokes that the food didn't make much difference. Everyone had a fine evening and our comfortable, but not fine, home received many words of praise."[18]

Aull did employ a maid periodically to give Luanna some much-needed relief. Mamma Sally wrote all the society news and a weekly women's column for the *Democrat* from home and had to spend a considerable amount of time on the telephone gathering information. As a result, she was able to keep readers informed of every meeting of such groups as the Busy Matrons, the Pleasant Hill Korky Kookers, the Harmony Needle Club, and the Victory Merry Woodsman Girls.

The Aulls grew very fond of the women who helped with the household chores over the years. Once, a teenage girl they employed taught fourteen-year-old Genevieve to drive the car "unknown to the Missus and the Boss, who considered her too young to drive," Madeleine recollected nearly fifty years later. "It was all done surreptitiously, and by the time they knew about it, Genevieve was a good driver." Unknowingly, the housekeepers also provided some comic relief along the way. When a rumor floated about town that Aull was having serious financial prob-

lems, their maid was stopped on the street one day. "Is it so that the Aulls are going broke?" the curious person asked. "I don't know," she replied, "but their icebox is full of food."[19] And Luanna liked to tell the following story:

> [The maid] was very interested in Betty getting ready to enter the university. There was the usual bustling about, packing suitcases, hatboxes and trunk. The maid was right in the middle of the scurrying around. Finally Betty was off, and we set about getting the house in order. Along in the afternoon she suddenly commented, "Betty must be at the end of her destitution, now!" We agreed, as we tucked away a hearty laugh for Arthur at suppertime. After some merriment, he said: "Ole Betts may be at the end of her destitution, but mine will continue for another four years."[20]

THE GIRLS GO OFF TO COLLEGE

All three Aull girls attended the University of Missouri. Madeleine wanted to study journalism, but her father advised against it. "You've no flair for newspapering," he said. "Take a liberal arts course."[21] Madeleine received a bachelor of science degree in education and a lifetime certificate to teach from the university in 1919. She taught high school history in Iowa and Kansas City, where she met and married Carl Van Hafften, an insurance man, in 1923. After living in St. Louis, Los Angeles, Chicago, Pittsburgh, and New York, she returned to Lamar in 1942 to assist her father with the *Democrat*.

Genevieve left the University of Missouri after a year to marry Garrett Noyes, owner and operator of the West Side Bakery in Lamar. They moved to Springfield, Missouri, where he took a position with Swift and Company. Genevieve presented Aull with his only two grandchildren, Nancy and Luanna. The first boy in the family, born to Luanna Noyes Martin, was named in honor of his great-grandfather after the editor's death. Genevieve and Garrett later operated a hardware store at Mount Vernon, Missouri, for seventeen years.

Upon entering the University of Missouri in 1926, Betty specialized in chemistry and biology with the hope of becoming a laboratory technician. "After two years at MU, I found I couldn't get this training," she explained. "Dad said he didn't know enough about national advertising and wanted to learn more about it, so I changed my major to journalism." To help facilitate her degree change, Aull wrote a letter to Walter Williams, still dean of the school of journalism. Aull considered Williams an old friend; the two had known each other for some twenty-five years. Williams arranged two special courses in national advertising for the editor's daughter and personally oversaw her progress.[22]

During her one year in the journalism school, Betty Aull met Stan White, president of the journalism student body and a fellow advertising major. "It was the romance of the campus," she said. "There was a bridge that ran over a small stream and that's where journalism students would go when they fell in love to seal their engagement. We went there and had our engagement kiss."[23] They graduated in 1930, in the throes of the Great Depression. While Stan looked for a suitable job to support a wife, Betty went to work for her father selling advertising and doing some reporting.

Their marriage was delayed even further when Betty nearly lost her life in a January 1932 car accident. She and a friend, H. D. (Tige) McDaniel, overseer of the Lamar Mills, were en route to a quail supper in Riverton, Kansas, when a truck carrying nine thousand pounds of condensed milk broadsided their Model A Ford at an intersection in Carthage, Missouri. McDaniel was killed, and Betty sustained a serious contusion to the brain, a broken collarbone, and a hole torn through her cheek. The Aulls were eating dinner that Saturday evening when the call came from McCune-Brooks Hospital in Carthage. "You and her mother must come at once!" said the caller, who would reveal only that McDaniel and their daughter had been in a wreck. Luanna jumped up from the table, threw a cloak on over her house dress, and the two set off on the twenty-four-mile trip. "Not a word was said, during that drive, which neither will ever forget," Aull wrote two days later. "It was a time too full of dreadful suspense for words."[24]

Betty's recuperation took eighteen months, during which she spent time with Madeleine in Los Angeles. Stan, meanwhile, was working in St. Louis as advertising manager for the James Kearney Company, a manufacturer of telephone and electric line supplies. They were married in February 1934 at the home of Genevieve and Garrett Noyes in Springfield, with only a few friends and relatives present. Although the story in the *Democrat* indicated that the bride and groom and her sisters had arranged the wedding on short notice, Aull had been directly involved in the planning. "Dad said I couldn't be married in Lamar because everybody who ever took the paper would think they had a right to come to the wedding," Betty explained. "They thought we were kind of their property. Dad said we'd have to rent Memorial Hall and it would just be a mess."[25]

AULL'S OTHER PLEASURES

Aside from his family and the newspaper, Aull's greatest pleasures in life came from relaxing with the family dog and tooling about town in his roadsters. He drove nothing but Chevrolets, first a green roadster and then a yellow one. He thought the bright colors would help protect Betty, who was still working for him. She recalled: "Every Tuesday, I had to go to Iantha, Liberal, and Mindenmines and cover those towns for him. On another day I went to Jasper and Sheldon. On another day, Golden City. With me on the road like that, he wanted a car everybody knew in case there was trouble. So he said that's why he bought such wild colors. Everyone would know it was Arthur Aull's car and his daughter."[26]

Aull and Luanna liked to put the car's top down and go for a long ride every evening, weather permitting. They often parked along a woodsy road, where one night they were spotted by a man who recognized the car but couldn't discern its occupants. The man came into the *Democrat* office the next morning to report the incident: "Arthur, I hate to tell you this, but your daughter is parking," he said, "and she's staying there pretty long." Aull responded, "Well, I hate to disappoint you, but that's my wife and me." The next time the Aulls were parked on the road, the man snuck up on the car. "It *is* you, Arthur," he said embarrassingly.[27]

When not driving about the countryside, Aull liked to curl up at home with either Mr. Wu or Tippy. Mr. Wu was a beautiful red chow Betty had acquired as a puppy. A large pen was built for him outside and a special door installed, giving him full run of the house and much of the yard. Unfortunately, Mr. Wu suffered from a severe case of eczema and eventually was taken to a noted dog specialist who advised that he be put to sleep. Of the thousands of articles Aull wrote during his lengthy career, his eulogy of Mr. Wu touched more readers than any scandalous story ever did. He concluded: "And for a long time, as we enter the door of the house there will be a reflex expectancy of

Mr. Wu, eager, pleased, his fine ears pointed upward and his soft eyes shining with love, there to greet us. Then there will be the sudden awakening to put the vagrant reflex of anticipation away and the pang that follows it."[28]

Madeleine's brother-in-law, an amateur painter living in New York, asked for a snapshot of Mr. Wu and proceeded to produce a nearly life-size oil painting of the dog. The picture was presented to the Aull family at Christmas, three months after the dog's death. "As we look at it there in its place on the wall," Aull wrote, "it seems so life-like that we almost feel as if we ought to walk up to it, pat it and talk to it!"[29]

Unlike the pedigreed and beautiful Mr. Wu, Tippy arrived at the Aull household as a not-too-handsome stray. He bided his time until Mr. Wu's death, when he became the number one dog. Tippy endeared himself to Aull by following him everywhere. He would rest on the sidewalk outside the *Democrat* office, or he would lay in a large wastebasket at the editor's feet. Dogs ran loose everywhere in Lamar and trampled many of the gardens, causing the city council in 1944 to enact an ordinance that all be penned. City Marshal Dee Bass informed Aull that this meant Tippy, too. "Other people will see him," Bass told him, "and they'll say, 'Arthur Aull's dog ain't any better than my dog. Why can't he come downtown?' " Aull abided by the ordinance, but reported, "It was awful lonesome when we got down to the square Monday morning because of the absence of the dogs." The ordinance was lifted six weeks later due to the cooperation of the city's dog owners, although each dog had to wear a license.[30]

When Tippy died in 1946, it made the front page of the *Democrat*. As with Mr. Wu five years earlier, the story produced a great many letters and sympathy cards. "Our little dog, Tippy, breathed his last Friday night," Aull wrote. "We went out to see Tippy Friday morning. He was very silent but apparently he was not suffering. But when we got up Saturday morning, the Missus came in and in a burst of tears, she told us Tippy was gone. . . . The gallant and faithful heart is stilled forever. But we shall always remember Tippy and may God bless his white and shining soul!!"[31]

8

CHANGING OF THE GUARD

Probably the writings of no other small town editor in Missouri have been more widely copied than have those of Arthur Aull. Atchison, Kans., has its Ed Howe, another editor who believed in calling a spade nothing but a spade. Troy, Kans., had its Sol Miller, another of the same ilk. Sarcoxie had its own Bernard Finn. Each of them was so much a part of his community that it was impossible to think of the editor, without also thinking of his hometown—and vice versa. So it was with Arthur Aull, his Lamar Democrat and Lamar itself. He had so linked them together that they have become known to thousands who never knew the editor, personally, or were ever anywhere near the town in which he printed his paper. They knew him for a small town editor who was "different;" an editor who detested hypocrisy, make-believe, artificiality, and the trite, moth-eaten stereotyped methods of handling of news and editorials.

—Carthage *(Mo.)* Evening Press, *May 10, 1948*

Decades of seventy-hour workweeks began to catch up with Arthur Aull in 1942. The first sign of trouble occurred when he returned to the *Democrat* office one Sunday afternoon after attending the funeral of Edwin Moore, the prominent Lamar attorney. He suddenly found himself without sight or a sense of direction, a condition that he likened to a "blind dog in the meat market." The editor stumbled out the door, managed to start for home in his yellow Chevrolet roadster, and promptly ran into the back of a parked car. He then set out on foot, walking through several yards and gardens before realizing he was lost. A kindly townsman found the editor, loaded him into his truck, and took him home.[1]

Aull visited an eye specialist who insisted that he sell the roadster and refrain from crossing the street in heavy traffic. Unknown to Aull at the time, though, was that the loss of vision signaled a more serious disorder than poor eyesight. He was in the early stages of arteriosclerosis, a hardening and thickening of the arteries. His workload had been heavier than usual that month with the loss of two employees to the armed forces. Madeleine Aull Van Hafften, his oldest daughter, was living in New York at the time with her husband, Carl. She came home to Lamar at once to help out until Aull could find "something better."[2]

Although Madeleine had not been permitted to study journalism in college, she received a four-year newspaper education from her father upon her return to Lamar in 1942. Among other things, he taught her not to print funeral home death notices word for word but to "dig out the facts and find out why the person died and all the circumstances." He also taught her to interview without taking any notes except for names, dates, and addresses. This system often resulted in inaccuracies, or at least differences of opinion as to what transpired. Aull instructed Madeleine that every complaint—provided it was signed—was to be published.[3]

With the assistance of his loyal daughter, to whom he was now dictating most of his stories, Aull continued his normal schedule until his health started deteriorating rapidly in 1946. His family and doctors finally convinced him to visit the famed Mayo Clinic, where he expected that little could be done for him except being placed on "another fancy starvation diet." The prognosis wasn't as bad as expected. Aull suffered from a kidney disorder, caused by "having worked too hard and too strenuously throughout his lifetime." He was advised to rest at home for six weeks to two months, avoiding the "clatter of the office and the irritations and interruptions attendant on the newspaper business."[4]

The rest was short-lived. Two weeks later, Aull was back at the office despite the objections of his wife and family. "But I feel better here and I will continue to stick around a good part of the time," he told his readers in November 1946. Aull did make one concession: he named

Madeleine assistant editor due to her "damned good" performance during his nine-day trip to the Mayo Clinic. She was surprised; she had hoped that someday he might make her a reporter.[5]

By February 1947, Aull's failing health did not allow him to visit the *Democrat* office even for a short time. A severe kidney flare-up resulted in a week-long stay at Barnes Hospital in St. Louis the next month. From his hospital bed he scrawled the following note to Madeleine: "Dear Honkie: Do a good job on the paper. My room is costing twelve dollars a day!"[6] Aull lived the last year of his life confined to his home, where he died of a heart attack and thrombosis at 11:30 P.M. on Friday, May 7, 1948. He was seventy-five.

Hours after her father's death, Madeleine hastened to the *Democrat* office; with tears streaming down her face, she wrote a seventy-column-inch tribute to her father for Saturday's paper. To those who knew Arthur Aull, it was no surprise that the *Democrat* put out an issue shortly after his death. He made the request himself, when he wasn't expected to live much longer. He insisted the paper publish on the day of his funeral as well. As for a will, he never felt one was necessary. He and his wife jointly owned everything, including the *Democrat.* His only stipulation was that the masthead of the paper be changed to show Luanna as publisher and Madeleine as editor.[7]

The family planned to hold a memorial service for Aull at the Konantz Funeral Home, but at the urging of Mayor Carrol Combs and the Lamar Chamber of Commerce they agreed to use the larger Memorial Hall. City officials maintained that because Aull "belonged to the community, his funeral should be made a community affair, in order that all could join in the final tribute."[8] Combs ordered all businesses in Lamar closed the afternoon of Monday, May 10, to honor the deceased editor.

More than five hundred people turned out for the funeral that day. Judge John Flanigan, of Carthage, Missouri, and one of Aull's closest friends, gave the eulogy. "The death of Arthur Aull has cost Lamar its foremost citizen," he said. "Journalism has lost one of its brightest stars and truth has lost a loyal citizen." Flanigan also read Aull's "A Creed of Life," published in the *Democrat* on July 14, 1921. The funeral's most poignant moment came at the end when Nell Casement, who managed the paper's twelve carrier boys, directed them in the removal of the great mass of flowers for the trip to the cemetery.[9] Aull was buried in Lamar's Lake Cemetery, next to his father.

TRIBUTES TO ARTHUR AULL

Telegrams of condolence and admiration for the late editor were delivered to his home and the *Democrat* office throughout Saturday, Sunday, and Monday. The Columbia Press Service relayed messages from President Truman and Missouri's congressional delegation. All were laudatory, though some more so than others. Republican Congressman Marion Bennett, from Aull's district, said Aull was "a worthy partisan political adversary who added much interest to political campaigns." However, Bennett added, Aull had "a unique talent for libel and slander." Another Missouri congressman, Republican Dewey Short, called Aull "a hard-hitting American and fighter for what he thought to be right."[10]

A more revealing indication of the public's regard for Aull came from his primary competitors—the other newspapers of Lamar and Barton County. All were highly complimentary. Under a headline that read "A Great Editor Is Dead," the *Golden City Herald* noted, "Arthur Aull brought Lamar into national prominence. Arthur Aull would have brought any small town where he might have lived into prominence. He was admired, he was hated, he was respected." The *Liberal News* also paid homage to the now-famous country editor: "To write the facts as he saw them was the aim from which he never deviated. His memory was phenomenal. Many still relate with awe how he would listen to lengthy speeches, not take a single note, then go back to his desk and write his story, quoting people exactly. Often sneered at and threatened with lawsuits, sometimes even set upon bodily, Aull nevertheless stayed with his ship of 'facts,' no matter how prominent the citizen at whose feet chips fell."[11]

The greatest tribute, though, came from Gene Crawford, publisher of the other daily paper in town, the *Lamar Republican*. Despite the many misspellings and typographical errors, the editorial puts Aull's career into historical perspective:

> Arthur Aull published the news as he saw it, without fear or favor to either friend or foe. His best friend would suffer in the pitilesss [*sic*] glare of the searchlight of publicity, handled by Aull as well as his worst enemy. In Mr. Aulls [*sic*] code there was no extenuating circumstances. News was news and was printed verbatim, holding no punches and camoflaging [*sic*] no facts in conventional language. He was ex-

travagantly praised and bitterly criticized, but read by and and [*sic*] sundry.

In his hey day [*sic*], he dominated the politics of the County and ran the town of Lamar. His religion, if any was a personal matter. Popular opinion says he was an Athiest [*sic*]. He lived by the sword and died as far as is known stanchly [*sic*] holding to his convictions. He asked favors of no man and extended none.

In the early years of Mr. Aulls career, there were quite a few editors of Mr. Aulls type, but they were passing then. The old school, went to press with a six shooter on their desk and wore their fighting clothes everyday. A few changed their editorial style to fit the changing times, but Mr. Aull stayed with his style after all others had died or changed[,] earning an unique position in the newspaper world by the style that became as far as is known, his own.

The writer has a wide acquaintance with the members of his profession and to the best of my knowledge, Arthur Aull is the last of his kind. The species is extinct. Increased post office supervision, more stringent libel laws, adoption of a newspapers [*sic*] code [of] ethics, by most newspapers, killed off most editorial comment such as Mr. Aulls, but he clung to his style after all others had quit.

His undeniable brilliance, his adroitnes [*sic*] at political maneuvering, and his political connections as well as his dominant personality kept him out of damage suits that would have ruined 99 out of 100 newspapers.

Arthur Aull is dead. His species is extinct. Over the country, there may crop up occasional imitators of Aulls, but they will always be imitators. They will not have the combinations of brains and luck to get away with the uninhibited publishing that Aull managed with ease. His enemies rejoice, his friends sorrow, but no one can ever really fill his shoes.[12]

THE FAMILY CARRIES ON

Luanna Aull assumed the role of publisher, but day-to-day operation of the *Democrat* was left to Madeleine as the new editor. The eldest daughter, who took to calling herself "Pee Wee Yours Truly," struggled to carry on the Aull tradition for five years until her brother-in-law, Stan White, arrived in 1953 to become advertising manager. In addition to a four-year stint in the U.S. Navy during World War II, White had served as advertising manager of the *Hope* (Ark.) *Star,* sales manager of a radio station in Oklahoma City, and manager of a radio station in Peoria, Illinois. Luanna announced his appointment herself in a front-page story:

> It has been my sincere desire, and that of my late husband, Arthur Aull, that the paper remain in the hands of the Aull family. My daughter, Madeleine, has done a fine job in carrying the torch laid down by her father.
>
> But as the town has grown and the potential of the paper increased, she has become increasingly aware of the fact that she stands in need of loyal assistance, particularly, in the field of advertising, for which she has little taste and less professional training.
>
> We both are therefore happy to announce that my son-in-law, Stanley E. White, has agreed to come to Lamar to provide this assistance.
>
> Madeleine will occupy her present position as editor, setting the policy of the paper and handling all of the news. Stan will become the advertising manager. As to the handling of the business and mechanics in connection with the operation, the two will function on a partnership basis.[13]

The move enabled Madeleine to concentrate solely on her reporting and writing. Sister Betty, while not a full-time employee, handled much of the society news and helped out in the office. Although the Whites added to the paper's payroll, the partnership was a financial success. Just ten months after Stan and Betty came to town, the *Democrat* could afford to buy out a nagging competitor, the daily *Lamar Journal.* This meant that Lamar, finally, was a one-newspaper town.[14]

The *Democrat* under Madeleine's editorship looked much like Aull's paper, except for some improved typography and the inclusion of photographs. She scoured the town for news, just as he had, always complaining about the lack thereof. She faithfully followed his practice of disregarding the traditional rules of privacy, even running the story of her own divorce on the front page of the *Democrat* in 1951. Despite her mighty attempt to run the *Democrat* in the same manner the "Boss" had, "Pee Wee Yours Truly" was never quite sure she measured up. In 1965, on the seventeenth anniversary of his death, she wrote, "It's a long long time but his 'presence' is still keenly felt in the Democrat office and each night we pray that from on high he will approve of our puny effort toward getting out the paper."[15]

Mamma Sally continued to write her weekly women's column until 1964 and keep up with local and national affairs. She was observed intently reading the evening edition of the *Kansas City Star* shortly before her death at the age of ninety-five on April 18, 1968. With seventy-five-year-old Madeleine and Stan in declining health, the *Democrat* was sold to Missouri Secretary of State James Kirkpatrick and his son, Don, for $160,000 on November 1, 1972.[16]

The sale briefly rekindled national media interest in the Aulls, as a story written by a *Chicago Daily News* assistant city editor appeared in such newspapers as the *Los Angeles Times, Memphis Commercial Appeal, Cincinnati Enquirer,* and *Miami Herald.* The author, Rob Warden, a native Missourian, wrote: "In their long stewardship of the Democrat, stretching over the 20th Century, the Aulls brought the feisty little paper to national prominence (especially when a Lamar native son, Harry Truman, was in the White House), and last month, when the paper was sold to new owners, a small but lively chapter in journalism history ended."[17]

ARTHUR AULL IN RETROSPECT

Without question, Arthur Aull was an atypical country editor. He didn't set type or run the presses. He spent as little time as possible soliciting job work and advertising. He wasn't particularly active in his state's press association, which may explain his exclusion from the Missouri Newspaper Hall of Fame.[18] He disregarded most of the traditional rules of journalism. He put out six issues per week in a town that was one of the nation's smallest to support a daily newspaper, let alone two. He wrote almost all of the copy himself and seldom used any syndicated "boiler plate" material.

As the primary writer for a daily newspaper, he worked eleven to twelve hours a day, seven days a week, with virtually no time off for vacations. After his death in 1948, a friend estimated that Aull had written eighty-five million words—about five thousand every day—as editor of the *Democrat.* His stories were amusing, disturbing, even vulgar at times. Many told of misfortune and death. Some were preposterous. But they all contained a sensational element, something his readers could gossip about. He defended the scandalous nature of the *Democrat* time and time again, claiming he was merely presenting the facts as he knew them. He was quick to point out that although people might object to his brand of journalism, they read his paper anyway. He believed that if a particular issue of the *Democrat* didn't contain anything of a striking nature, it was immediately discarded.

Aull responded to all expressions of dissatisfaction, even informal ones, with a word or two in the *Democrat*. Those who found fault with his policy of printing everything were consistently rebuked, though not by name. In 1908, for example, he scolded a critic: "As long as people denounce a newspaper for printing scandals and then walk four blocks to borrow a copy of the paper that has the scandal in it, the force of public sentiment isn't going to be very strong in favor of a press that prints long stories about the prospect for North Dakota wheat and makes no mention of the woman who ran off with her friend's husband."[19]

The writers who profiled Aull in the 1940s marveled at his ability to remain in business year after year without being lynched or run out of town on a rail. One, Horace Blaise, who spent two weeks in Lamar in 1946 observing how people regarded the *Democrat* and its policies, wondered how he stayed out of the poorhouse. "Arthur Aull's Democrat is an object lesson in how not to run a country paper and make it pay," he wrote in the *St. Louis Post-Dispatch*. Nevertheless, Blaise reported that Aull cleared a respectable eight thousand dollars in 1945, his property was unmortgaged and worth fifty thousand dollars, and the *Democrat* had one of the best-equipped newspaper offices around.[20]

Circulation figures support Aull's assertion that scandal sold newspapers. The *Democrat*'s circulation exceeded the population of Lamar for most of his editorship. The paper was widely read throughout Barton County and could boast of subscribers in all forty-eight states. A few irate readers canceled their subscriptions along the way, but as Aull liked to point out, they usually managed to borrow someone else's copy.

Aull's practice was to print every letter of complaint received, provided it was signed. Some were blistering, of course, but the majority dealt with misquotes, mistaken attribution, and other inaccuracies. Aull delighted in publishing letters to the editor, especially the scathing ones, because his readers enjoyed him "catching hell" more than anything. Still, a forty-eight-year examination of the *Democrat* turned up only a small number of letters that flayed Aull, indicating minimal dissatisfaction from readers.

The community unequivocally accepted his idea of news coverage and allowed him to run a profitable business for the simple reason that he was fair, honest, and consistent. Although a few readers referred to "lies" in stories, Aull's honesty was never questioned. He didn't obtain stories by deceptive means. The community knew that any divorce, rape, fight, juvenile crime, or attempted suicide would be brought to its attention in that afternoon's *Democrat.* No one was above publication, not Aull, not his family, not his closest friends. He held his three daughters to a higher standard of conduct knowing most of Barton County was watching. Betty Aull White said they "had to walk the line, because if we ever did anything we really were put on the front page."[21] Had he neglected to publicize any of his own embarrassments, the community would not have so readily accepted the scathing stories about them in the *Democrat* every day.

Aull was praised profusely by the big-city newspapers and magazines that deemed him worthy of a feature story. His reporting was described as "straight-forward," "ripsnorting," and "ingenuous."[22] His unabashed disregard for a person's right to privacy, however, received little mention. To Aull, literally everything was newsworthy. He didn't believe in safeguarding anyone's privacy and showed little compassion toward those who may have been harmed by one of his sensational stories. He identified rape victims and juvenile offenders by name. He revealed the most gruesome details of suicides and exposed those who had attempted suicide. He publicized the most embarrassing details in divorce proceedings and sex crimes. He essentially exploited every tragic situation with little regard for the individual or family involved.

During their many trips to Lamar, the national media failed to pick up on the more valid explanation for Aull's tell-all brand of journalism. It was one that he had explained three or four times for his readers. Publishing a daily newspaper in a town the size of Lamar necessitated that he include virtually every single happening—newsworthy or not—in the paper. He insisted that all news be local, that syndicated material not be used as filler. Consequently, Aull would sit in the office some days with no deaths, marriages, divorces, fights, lawsuits, or even a crap game to write about and four empty pages staring him in the face.

Aull put out more than fourteen thousand issues as editor of the *Democrat,* taking only a handful of days off. Despite the national write-ups, he felt a lack of appreciation at times. The people of Lamar took the *Democrat* for granted, seldom acknowledging the long hours he was putting in on their behalf. He compared himself to the family cook: "She works hard getting the meal ready. It is eaten in a few minutes.

Then she must gather up and wash the dishes. When the paper is gotten out, after a hard day's work, folks pick it up, glance at it and toss it aside and say there's nothing in it. Then it's tear up the forms and start all over again on next day's paper."[23]

Before the national media catapulted him into the spotlight, Aull tried to emulate William Allen White and Ed Howe, two country editors known coast to coast. White's 1896 editorial in the *Emporia Gazette,* "What's the Matter with Kansas?" sprung him to fame. Aull tried to copy White's formula in the 1920s with a series of editorials called "What's the Matter with the Farm?" "What's the Matter?" and "What's the Matter with the Courts?" but those failed to bring him any national acclaim.[24]

Aull never commented in the *Democrat* on his successes and failures. His family was not privy to his innermost thoughts and feelings either. He seldom talked about himself. "He never said anything about all those great write-ups," recalled his daughter Betty. "There was never any mention made." His wife, Luanna, wondered after his death if he felt disappointment because "his national recognition came from his witticisms, his human nature stories and his frank reporting, rather than from his editorials."[25]

Little insight can be gained from Aull's "A Creed of Life." Walter Williams's "Journalist's Creed" may have served as the inspiration. With his own "Creed," a rambling, 635-word essay, Aull made yet another attempt to become a national figure. But like the "What's the Matter?" editorials, the creed was not picked up by other papers.

The national media did accord Aull some renown for his "uncanny prescience in national and international affairs." Even before the *Literary Digest's* flawed poll led it to the embarrassing prediction that Kansas Governor Alfred Landon would defeat Franklin Roosevelt in the 1936 presidential election, Aull was announcing that the magazine's poll-taking method "no longer constitutes a dependable test." Many of Aull's prognostications did come true. In 1935, for example, he declared that "the world is moving towards another great war." And in January 1941 he predicted that before the end of the year America would be forced to enter a second world war.[26]

But many of Aull's predictions turned out to be wrong, and these errors were ignored by the national media in their feature stories about the editor. Just two and a half months before a cease-fire signaled the end of World War I, Aull told readers the war was "pretty sure to last two more years." Ten years later, after Herbert Hoover won a landslide victory for the presidency, he predicted that Hoover would be reelected in 1932 and perhaps again in 1936. In 1938, Aull cautioned that America's refusal to prepare for war would cause it to be "crushed between German-lead [*sic*] Europe and Japanese directed Asia."[27]

Arthur Aull was simply a country newspaper editor who followed his own code of ethics for forty-eight years without any sort of modification to reflect the changing times. His species, without a doubt, is extinct. Country editors still exist, but today they are called community journalists. They still work seventy-hour weeks and struggle to sell enough advertising to pay expenses and turn a small profit. They still think of clever campaigns to build up the circulation base. They still calm down the occasional irate subscriber. They still give generously of their time and money to projects that will benefit the community. And many still buck the policies and procedures recommended by the schools of journalism.

But for the most part, the personalities of today's editors are not reflected in their papers. Wary of causing irreparable damage to their livelihood, few feel the freedom to print the absolute truth in every circumstance. Few publicize every private fact in their community. And few ever receive the small measure of fame Arthur Aull was afforded for his sensational brand of journalism. It wasn't unique to him; he just did it longer than anyone else and survived.

APPENDIX A

AULL BIOGRAPHICAL INFORMATION

BORN: November 18, 1872, in Daviess County, Kentucky, near Knotts-ville.

PARENTS: William Aull (January 16, 1848–June 22, 1930) and Mary Pool Aull (1850–May 31, 1876).

EDUCATION: Attended the rural school at Nashville, Missouri, and Fort Scott (Kansas) Normal School, dates unknown.

WIFE: Luanna Belle Turnbull Aull (April 6, 1873–April 18, 1968).

MARRIAGE: March 22, 1896, at Nashville, Missouri.

OCCUPATION: Teacher, dates unknown, at Mindenmines, Missouri. Editor and publisher, *Lamar Democrat,* 1900-1948.

CHILDREN: Madeleine Aull Van Hafften (November 20, 1896–November 21, 1977), Genevieve Aull Noyes Turrentine (September 30, 1903–), and Betty Aull White (January 14, 1908–).

RELIGION: Agnostic. Wife and children attended the Presbyterian church.

POLITICS: Democrat. Elected surveyor of Barton County in 1896. Appointed postmaster of Lamar from August 1915 to January 1924. Elected to Lamar School Board in 1917 and 1920.

HOBBIES: Entertaining at home; reading poems, novels, and historical works.

DOGS: A pedigreed red chow, Mr. Wu; a stray, Tippy.

MEMBERSHIPS: Lamar Shakespeare Club, Lamar Chamber of Commerce, Lake Cemetery Association.

DEATH: May 7, 1948, in Lamar, Missouri.

BURIAL: Lake Cemetery in Lamar, Missouri.

APPENDIX B

AULL'S "A CREED OF LIFE"

Lamar Democrat, JULY 14, 1921; REPRINTED MAY 11, 1948

I would do my best to look upon myself as I do upon others. I would seek to remember that while a man may have been unjust to me and said dispiteful things of me and mine, I would best serve myself, by striving to remember, that I too, had frequently been unjust, and this man's offense was perhaps no greater than mine. I would strive to know the world as it is and adapt myself to its resistless and flowing life.

I would remember, that while men are envious, greedy, self-seeking and filled with the virus of a small ego, that it was nature and not they, who is to blame. Having been placed here, in a universe, where every living thing is faced with the potential necessary to fight for its right to live, we could not expect these children of the cosmos slime to be otherwise than what they are. I would look impartially as I could upon my own secret thoughts and see if, in fact, I was not envious, self-seeking, and mindful of myself, before I seriously thought of others.

I would remember that other men might have greater deserts than I, that there were among them, those who had superior skill, and who were more able, than I, to cope with the forces against which we strive to live and have. I would confess to myself, that others not only had much better places of vantage than I possessed from which to relinquish it to another, but I would try to remember, that if I had one of their coignes of superior chance, I would not willingly relinquish it to another, but I would be inclined to use it to its reasonable utmost.

So if another man rides, where I walk, I will get all that I can out of the walking, bide the day, when I hope I may ride, and not burden those about me with useless complaints. I will not whine and call the world unfair. I may suffer from slander. The barbs of malice may fly,

ever and anon, from the tongues of those who are idle, envious, cha-
grined at their own unmet desires. But I will strive not to reply in kind,
for little as I know of life, I have already learned, that he who makes a
bed of lies, of malice and foolish envy, it is himself, and not another,
who, in the end, must sleep in its prickly and tormenting filth.

I would strive to keep an open mind and I would school myself, not
to be ashamed to say, I was wrong. I would realize that, while I came
into the world, in the grip of forces far beyond my puny and fleeting
control, yet it was none the less my duty, at all times, to give an account
of my own efforts, my conduct, my life. I would not pull aside my gar-
ments from the life about me and say, All is foolishness, sin and corruption. Rather would I enter into it still more deeply, rather would I study
it, rather would I seek to understand the currents of its resistless and
endless stream, for only in understanding is there wisdom or real worth.

I would remind myself that while my burdens might seem heavy and
galling, yet there were myriads of men, who bore still heavier loads, in
proportion to their strength, and that the time to evade a burden is before you accept it and not after you take it on. I would seek as far as I
might to divest myself of false pride, for we easily underrate others and
unduly enhance ourselves. After having done my best, I would seek to
accept the results whatever they might be, knowing that I need not be
ashamed.

NOTES

CHAPTER 1

1. "The Comment of President Truman."
2. "Arthur Aull Funeral Tomorrow; Editor Who Pulled No Punches."
3. Charles B. Driscoll, *The Life of O. O. McIntyre,* 20.
4. John R. Cauley, "Aull Prints All the News," 8.
5. "Biography and Comments on the Death of William Aull."
6. Ibid.
7. Madeleine Aull Van Hafften, "Arthur Aull Is Dead"; White interview by author, March 16, 1994.
8. Luanna Aull, "A Word to the Voters"; Van Hafften, "Arthur Aull Is Dead."
9. Luanna Aull, "Gleanings," July 21, 1960.
10. Luanna Aull, "A Tribute to a Wonderful Man."
11. Reba Young, *Down Memory Lane,* 53.
12. "Oliver P. Turnbull."
13. Luanna Aull, "Gleanings," November 19, 1959; Virginia Faulkner, ed., *Roundup: A Nebraska Reader,* 266.
14. White interview by author, March 16, 1994.
15. Luanna Aull, "A Tribute to a Wonderful Man."
16. Luanna Aull, "A Tribute to a Wonderful Man." Some accounts have placed the purchase price at fifty-five hundred dollars. Sally Foreman Griffith, *Home Town News: William Allen White and the Emporia Gazette,* 30.
17. "From The Lamar Democrat 25 Years Ago"; Luanna Aull, "A Tribute to a Wonderful Man."
18. Calder M. Pickett, *Ed Howe: Country Town Philosopher,* 187; H. V. Blaise, "Irrepressible Country Editor"; Luanna Aull, "A Tribute to a Wonderful Man."
19. Luanna Aull, "Gleanings," September 14, 1961.

20. Luanna Aull, "Gleanings," June 8, 1963; Luanna Aull, "A Tribute to a Wonderful Man."

21. Blaise, "Irrepressible Country Editor"; "Statement of the Ownership, Management, Circulation, Etc., Required by the Act of Congress of August 24, 1912"; Luanna Aull, "A Tribute to a Wonderful Man."

22. Rob Warden, "All the News That's Fit to Print (And a Little Something Extra) Down in Lamar, Missouri."

23. Marvin L. VanGilder, *The Story of Barton County*, 6.

24. "The Democrat Will Move."

25. "Story of West Barton Coal Field, Now Practically Dug Out, Reads Like a Legend of Gold"; "The Coal Fields Are Declining."

26. VanGilder, *The Story of Barton County*, 4. See also "Tiny Is Sour on Lamar."

CHAPTER 2

1. VanGilder, *The Story of Barton County*, 9.

2. "To the People of Barton County."

3. Jay E. House, "The Old Country Weekly," 25; Will Rose, "The Small-Town Newspaper Divorces Its Party," 314–15.

4. Griffith, *Home Town News*, 43.

5. *Carthage Evening Press*, January 31, 1902.

6. "Arthur Rozelle Near Death."

7. *Lamar Democrat*, August 16, 1900.

8. Barbara Cloud, *The Business of Newspapers on the Western Frontier*, 59. Square was a measure similar to the modern-day column inch, although the actual depth varied. According to Cloud, a square may have originally been based on two inches and a two-inch-wide column. Publishers sometimes defined their "square" specifically in terms of the numbers of lines, such as ten or twelve or sixteen. Twelve lines of nonpareil type (six-point type) made an inch, essentially a column inch.

9. "Who's Hurt?"

10. "Does It Love Them!"

11. "Clear Case of Robbery."

12. "Clear Case of Robbery"; *Lamar Industrial Leader*, July 26, 1901.

13. "A 'Pie' Combination."

14. *Lamar Democrat*, July 25, 1901.

15. "Wolf in Sheep's Clothing."

16. "Wolf in Sheep's Clothing"; *Lamar Industrial Leader*, August 2, 1901.

17. *Lamar Industrial Leader*, August 2, 1901.

18. *Lamar Industrial Leader*, August 9, 1901.

19. Ibid.

20. "No Relief"; *Jasper County Democrat,* August 7, 1901.

21. *Lamar Republican,* August 8, 1901; August 8, 1901.

22. "The Committee's Report."

23. "Result of the Investigation."

24. "Investigation Demanded."

25. "A Fake 'Letter'"; *Lamar Industrial Leader,* August 23, 1901.

26. "Put Up or Shut Up"; "Up to Rozelle."

27. William F. Swindler, *Problems of Law in Journalism,* 102, 105; Fredrick Seaton Siebert, *The Rights and Privileges of the Press,* 122.

28. "Charged With Libel"; *Lamar Industrial Leader,* September 20, 1901.

29. "Sharps and Flats," September 20, 1901.

30. "Who is the Ingrate?"

31. "Sharps and Flats," October 4, 1901.

32. *Lamar Democrat,* August 15, 1901.

33. "State vs. Arthur Aull."

34. "The Libel Cases."

35. "State vs. Arthur Aull."

36. "Birds of a Feather."

37. "The Libel Cases."

38. Ibid. Trial coverage from the *Lamar Industrial Leader* is not available. The holdings of the State Historical Society of Missouri are incomplete for the *Leader.*

39. "Verdict of Acquittal."

40. Ibid.

41. Reprinted in the *Golden City Free Press,* January 30, 1902.

42. "The Libel Cases."

43. Arthur Aull, "Advertising."

44. "Verdict of Acquittal"; "Democrats and Libel."

45. Reprinted in the *Lamar Republican,* April 24, 1902.

46. *Lamar Democrat,* November 19, 1903; "Mr. Rozelle Dead."

47. "As to Mr. Moore's Reply."

48. "Some Plain Talk"; "As to Mr. Moore's Note"; "Mr. Moore's Reply."

49. "Friends Bid Farewell to Hon. E. L. Moore"; "Lamar Loses Her Premier Lawyer and Citizen."

50. "The Attitude of the Democrat."

51. Rose, "The Small-Town Newspaper," 316.

52. *Lamar Democrat,* April 27, 1922.

CHAPTER 3

1. "The Yellow Press."

2. Ibid.

3. Frank Luther Mott, *American Journalism,* 541.

4. *Lamar Democrat,* September 16, 1909.

5. Charles Moreau Harger, "The Country Editor of To-Day," 90.

6. Charles Laurel Allen, *Country Journalism,* 90–91.

7. James Clifford Safley, *The Country Newspaper and Its Operation,* 9.

8. Mott, *American Journalism,* 539; See Michael Emery and Edwin Emery, *The Press and America,* 232. In the *Lamar Democrat,* see February 27, 1908; May 22, 1902; December 17, 1908; February 4, 1909; and August 3, 1911.

9. "Caught a Tigress"; "To Go to Hell vs. Don't Give a Damn."

10. "Bride a Giantess."

11. "Grim and Grisly."

12. Blaise, "Irrepressible Country Editor"; "He Shaved the President"; "Terrific Fight in Barber Shop."

13. White interview by author, July 6, 1992.

14. "A Country Editor Who Knows His Readers Want Life 'As Is'"; *Lamar Democrat,* July 31, 1902.

15. *Lamar Democrat,* October 27, 1921; "A Visitor Brings Us Back to Auld Lang Syne."

16. The *Lamar Leader* published a daily edition from 1895 to 1910. The *Lamar Republican* published a daily edition from 1932 to 1950; *N. W. Ayer and Son's American Newspaper Annual and Directory,* 580, 516.

17. Frank S. Popplewell, "Arthur Aull and The Lamar Democrat: A Study in Rural Missouri Journalism in the 1920's," 3.

18. *Lamar Democrat,* October 8, 1903; February 17, 1910.

19. Ibid., March 18, 1909; March 7, 1918.

20. Ibid., March 7, 1918.

21. Ibid., October 29, 1908.

22. "Mable Mott Marries Kewpie Kewps."

23. *Lamar Democrat,* September 1, 1904.

24. Ibid., January 20, 1910.

25. Ibid., September 12, 1929; November 6, 1934.

26. Ibid., October 15, 1937; Phil C. Bing, *The Country Weekly,* 69.

27. *Lamar Democrat,* February 15, 1917.

28. Ibid., January 20, 1921.

29. Richard Jones to Chad Stebbins, November 29, 1994; Warden, "All the News That's Fit to Print."

30. "Four Couples Granted Freedom"; "The Tragedies That Follow the Altar"; *Lamar Democrat,* May 29, 1902.

31. "Court Grants Nine Divorces"; Cauley, "Aull Prints All the News," 8.

32. "Several Men Freed from Matrimony."

33. "The Tragedies of Love."

34. "Monday Was Divorce Day."

35. "Still More Want Divorces."

36. "Ten Divorces Granted, Monday."

37. "It Was Divorce Day"; "Out of Ten Divorces, Nine Go to Women."

38. "The Day for the Divorces."

39. "The Tragedies That Follow the Altar."

40. "Thirteen Brief Stories of Ruined Marriages."

41. *Lamar Democrat*, April 11, 1933.

42. "Four Quit, Two Go Together."

43. "They Tell Their Marital Woes."

44. *Lamar Democrat*, September 20, 1917.

45. Ibid., March 21, 1929; August 14, 1934; January 12, 1934.

46. Ibid., March 12, 1935.

47. Ibid., March 21, 1929.

48. Ibid., May 5, 1936; January 3, 1936.

49. "Chas. B. Whalen Is Released."

50. "Dorothy Sullivan Told a Story Such As Was Never Before Told in a Barton County Court"; "Dorothy Sullivan Tells Her Story, Whallen Tells His"; "Jury Acquitted Whallen."

51. "Much Discussion of the Whallen Sodomy Case"; "Whalen Convicted, But Jury Let Him Off On a Fifty Dollar Fine and Costs."

52. "Charged With Attempted Rape of Three Year Old Girl"; "Charlie Slates Convicted of Illicit Relationships with Girl 10!"

53. Allen, *Country Journalism*, 98.

54. "An Eight Year Old Mail Robber"; "A Ten Year Old Burglar"; "A Boy Burglar"; "Thirteen Year Old Boy Dead Drunk."

55. "By Her Own Hand."

56. "Splattered Brains and Blood All Over His Three Children."

57. "Watching Two Men Die."

58. *Lamar Democrat*, July 16, 1925.

59. "The Most Horrible Wreck That Ever Occurred in Barton County."

60. "Miss Mae Hylton Under Surgeon's Knife"; "Jar of Stones Came From Patient's Gall Cyst"; "Has Been Tough on the Misses."

61. *Lamar Democrat*, August 27, 1914; "Country Editor"; and Blaise, "Irrepressible Country Editor."

62. Cauley, "Aull Prints All the News," 8.

63. *Lamar Democrat*, July 7, 1939.

64. Ibid.

65. Blaise, "Irrepressible Country Editor"; *Lamar Democrat*, December 17, 1925.

66. "Mark Sure Wants It Stopped."

67. "Speaking the Public Mind."

68. "Got Eddie's Baby's Age Wrong. For Such Awful Lie He's Sure We Have to Take Sleeping Powder."

69. "Miss Davidson Is Not Married."

70. "Well, We Say Too, What About These Warrants"; "We Pulled a Good One."

71. "Rev. Ward Takes Yours Truly to the Woodshed."

72. "Rev. Ward Takes Yours Truly to the Woodshed"; "Scorns a Cussin' Editor."

73. "Rev. Ward Feels That We Misrepresented the Pacifists and Are Unfair to Them"; "Rev. Ward Brings Us an Article from Zions Herald Declaring That Japan is Breaking."

74. "Mrs. Jackson Gets Into Our Wool"; "Don't Shoot the Fiddler, He's Doing His Best"; *Lamar Democrat,* August 19, 1920.

75. *Lamar Democrat,* November 12, 1903; September 8, 1910.

76. "Shoots Up Democrat Office."

77. Ibid.

78. Blaise, "Irrepressible Country Editor."

79. White interview by author, March 16, 1994.

80. "Mrs. Brooks Passionately Denies Circulating the Petition."

81. "We Certainly Got One Bloody Head at the Eversall House."

82. Don Eddy, "Ripsnorting News," 135; "We Certainly Got One Bloody Head at the Eversall House."

83. "Walter Kremp Sues The Democrat for Ten Thousand Dollars"; "Ten Thousand Dollar Suit Against Lamar Democrat Dismissed by Judge Hendricks."

84. "Martha Lamar Mother of Rex Sues Paper for Fifty Thousand."

85. "Yours Truly in a Crash—When It Rains It Just Naturally Pours"; "Lamar Case Dismissed."

86. "Arthur Aull Natureman."

87. "Cook's Evening Out."

88. Luanna Aull, "Gleanings," February 20, 1958.

89. "Cook's Evening Out."

90. Ibid.

91. "Truman Makes His Address to Ten Thousand."

92. Margaret Truman, *Harry S. Truman,* 186; "Truman Day a Wonderful Day."

93. "Under an Ozark Moon."

94. "We Get Another Write-Up"; "Two Distinguished Newspapermen from Chicago Spent Two Days in Lamar."

95. Cauley, "Aull Prints All the News," 8; "All the News," 52.

CHAPTER 4

1. "Career of John M. Harlow."
2. "Died at St. John's Hospital."
3. "Owens Had Long Criminal Record."
4. Ibid.; "Completes Lynch's Criminal Record."
5. "Completes Lynch's Criminal Record"; "Lynch Faced Five Year Term"; "Owens Had Long Criminal Record"; "Criminal Record of Man Hanged by Mob at Lamar."
6. "Inquest Develops the Evidence."
7. Whether Lynch had the gun hidden on his person when he was arrested or it was smuggled to him inside the jail would remain a mystery. "Sheriff J. M. Harlow Murdered."
8. Ibid.; "Romantic and Marvelous Story of Lynch's Escape."
9. "Romantic and Marvelous Story of Lynch's Escape."
10. Ibid.
11. "Sheriff Harlow Sleeps Among Old Neighbors"; "Died at St. John's Hospital."
12. "Romantic and Marvelous Story"; "Lynch is in the Butler Jail."
13. "Lynch is in the Butler Jail."
14. "Lynch Persisted in Staying to See His Wife."
15. "Warrants May Be Issued in Lamar Hanging"; "Sheriff Recognized Leaders of Mob that Hanged Jay Lynch."
16. "Seek Evidence on Mob"; "Lynch Brought to Lamar."
17. "Mob Hangs Slayer"; "Lynch Brought to Lamar."
18. "Lynch Brought to Lamar"; "Saved Women From Mob"; "Jay Lynch Gets Life Sentence."
19. "Mob Hangs Slayer"; "Sheriff Recognized Leaders."
20. "Mob Hangs Slayer"; "Lynch Brought to Lamar."
21. "Jay Lynch Gets Life Sentence"; "Lynch Brought to Lamar."
22. "Jay Lynch Gets Life Sentence"; "Lynch Brought to Lamar."
23. "Jay Lynch Gets Life Sentence."
24. "Sheriff Recognized Leaders."
25. "Lynch Hanged to an Elm Tree."
26. Ibid.; "Mob Hangs Slayer"; "Sheriff Recognized Leaders."
27. "Sheriff Recognized Leaders."
28. "Mob Hangs Slayer"; "A Mob Hangs Lynch at 3:45."
29. "Prosecutor Has Names of 9 Men in Lynch Mob"; "Lynch Hanged to an Elm Tree"; "Many Women in Mob that Hanged Slayer of Sheriff Harlow."
30. "A Mob Hangs Lynch at 3:45"; "Still Talk About Lynch."
31. White interview by author, March 16, 1994.

32. "Threatened to Lynch the Women"; "Saved Women from Mob"; "Threatened to Lynch the Women."

33. "Mob Hangs Slayer"; "Threatened to Lynch the Women."

34. "Sheriff Recognized Leaders"; "A Mob Hangs Lynch at 3:45."

35. "Many Women in Mob"; "Lynch's Body at Forest Park Cemetery."

36. "Saved Women from Mob"; "Mob Hangs Slayer"; "Seek Evidence on Mob."

37. "Seek Evidence on Mob." See also "Saved Women from Mob"; "Prosecutor Has Names."

38. "Governor Offers Prosecutor Aid in Lynch Hanging"; "Governor Asks Information"; "No Lynchers Ever Tried?"

39. "No Lynchers Ever Tried?"; Frank Shay, *Judge Lynch: His First Hundred Years,* 139, 151, 263, 274.

40. "Mob Enters Court and Hangs a Life Convict Sentenced Under Law Barring Death Penalty."

41. "Bolshevism in Missouri."

42. "The Lamar Lynching."

43. Reprinted in "Back Wash on the Lynch Hanging"; and "Talks Right Out Loud."

44. Reprinted in "Tells the Governor Where to Begin in Lynch Case"; "The Root of Lynching."

45. Reprinted in "Some Country Papers on the Lynch Hanging."

46. Ibid.

47. "He Says Hurrah for Lamar."

48. "Lynch Brought to Lamar"; "Threatened to Lynch the Women."

49. "Tries to Get the Facts."

50. "As to Punishing the Mob."

51. "Back Wash on the Lynch Hanging."

52. VanGilder, *The Story of Barton County,* 29.

53. "As to Punishing the Mob."

54. Thomas D. Clark, *The Southern Country Editor,* 228, 243–44.

55. James R. McGovern, *Anatomy of a Lynching: The Killing of Claude Neal,* x, 3.

56. "Death Penalty for Six Crimes"; "Gardner Signs Bill Restoring Death Penalty"; 1919 Laws of Missouri, 778–81.

57. "To Investigate Lynch Hanging"; "Jury Could Learn Nothing About Lynching."

58. "Lynch Trial Postponed"; "Mrs. Maude Lynch Acquitted."

59. "As to Punishing the Mob."

CHAPTER 5

1. Bing, *The Country Weekly*, 11.
2. *Lamar Democrat*, May 18, 1948.
3. *N. W. Ayer and Son's*, 466, 475; Blaise, "Irrepressible Country Editor"; "Pay!"
4. "Pay!"; "To Our Readers"; "Come Quick."
5. *Lamar Democrat*, January 9, 1908.
6. *N. W. Ayer and Son's*, 477.
7. *Lamar Democrat*, February 11, 1909; "Farewell, a Long Farewell"; "The Democrat Will Move."
8. "Who Will Get This Piano?"
9. "Miss Bartlett Awarded the Piano."
10. "History of the Piano Case."
11. "Miss Bartlett Awarded the Piano."
12. Ibid.
13. "History of the Piano Case."
14. Ibid.
15. "The Piano into Court."
16. Ibid.
17. "History of the Piano Case."
18. "Miss Bartlett Awarded the Piano."
19. "Miss Adams Wins."
20. "Five Hundred Dollars in Gold."
21. *N. W. Ayer and Son's*, 477, 504; "Five Hundred Dollars in Gold."
22. "The Leader Contest Closes"; *N. W. Ayer and Son's*, 503.
23. "Miss Isenhower Wins"; "A Word from Miss Isenhower"; "A Word from Mrs. Copeland."
24. In 1912 the *Democrat*'s weekly circulation was 3,993; its daily circulation was 1,002. Lamar's population (1910 Census) was 2,316. See *N. W. Ayer and Son's*, 503. In 1912 the *Gazette*'s weekly circulation was 1,350; its daily circulation was 3,534. Emporia's population (1910 Census) was 9,058. See *N. W. Ayer and Son's*, 311; "Miss Isenhower Wins."
25. *N. W. Ayer and Son's*, 582, 498, 533.
26. *Lamar Democrat*, September 2, 1915.
27. Ibid., May 30, 1918.
28. "To a Dollar and a Half a Year."
29. Harold U. Faulkner, *From Versailes to the New Deal*, 262, 264; William Allen White, *The Autobiography of William Allen White*, 610.
30. "Dr. Montgomery Was Arrested"; *Lamar Democrat*, November 24, 1921.
31. "Paper Lost on the Gold Awards."

32. "Rev. Jones Is for the Klan."

33. "A Klan Is Forming in Lamar"; "1000 Hear About the Ku Klux Klan."

34. "Round and Round Over Klan Meeting."

35. *Lamar Democrat,* July 5, 1923; "Klan Issues Its Paper at Mulberry."

36. "Klan to Make Demonstration in Lamar"; "Wow! Wow!! Wow!!!"

37. "They Heard the White Robed Klansman."

38. "Hot Klan Battle at Liberal."

39. "Lamar Has Her First Ku Klux Parade."

40. "Tear Gas Bomb at Ku Klux Meeting."

41. Arthur Aull, "Advertising."

42. Ibid.

43. Ibid.

44. "Story of a Great Store."

45. Griffith, *Home Town News,* 87. For an example of a front-page Harkless ad, see the front pages of the October 8, 1908, and November 19, 1908, *Lamar Democrat.* "Story of a Great Store."

46. "Toss Harkless Is Dead!"; "The End of 'Lamar's Great Store.'"

47. "A Mighty Cheap Press, Folder, Chases and Motor for Some Country Paper"; "A Bran New Paper This Week."

48. Aull, "Advertising."

49. *Lamar Democrat,* July 28, 1927; "How Would the Readers Answer This Question?"

50. "Merchants and Business Men Bring Christmas Greetings."

51. Eddy, "Ripsnorting News," 135, 136; Blaise, "Irrepressible Country Editor."

52. "Petition Presented to the Paper Asking That It Forbid the Mention of Beer, Whiskey and Other Alcoholic Drinks in the Advertisements."

53. "The Boys in Lamar Are Drinking Real Beer."

54. "The Case of a Good Man Enthralled by Liquor"; "Petition Presented to the Paper."

55. "Petition Presented to the Paper."

56. *Lamar Democrat,* December 4, 1934.

57. Ibid., July 28, 1933.

58. "Pepper and Salt," December 3, 1940.

59. "Here's the Story"; Blaise, "Irrepressible Country Editor."

60. Carroll Carroll, *None of Your Business: Or My Life with J. Walter Thompson,* ix; and Richard Morgan, *J. Walter Takeover: From Divine Right to Common Stock,* 17.

61. "Yours Truly Should Be in New York When You Read This."

62. Ibid.

63. "The Boss Says Flying in a Liner is Kinda Dull—But He Likes It That Way."

64. "Here's the Story."
65. Madeleine Aull Van Hafften, "A Middle Westerner on the Sidewalks of New York."
66. Luanna Aull, "Arthur Gets Posies."

CHAPTER 6

1. Luanna Aull, "Gleanings," February 7, 1957. The description came from Walter Mayes, a political acquaintance of Aull's. Eddy, "Ripsnorting News," 135–36.
2. *Lamar Democrat,* February 4, 1904.
3. *Official Manual of the State of Missouri for the Years 1915–1916,* 669.
4. "Here's What They Say."
5. Ibid.
6. "The Growth of the Lamar Post Office."
7. "The End for Familiar Lamar Character."
8. "The Growth of the Lamar Post Office."
9. "In Relation to the Lamar Public Schools."
10. "No Opposition."
11. "Statement in Regard to the Schoolboard."
12. Ibid.
13. "By the Skin of His Teeth."
14. "Unseen Committee Issues Statement"; "By the Skin of His Teeth."
15. "Personal Impressions of a Candidate."
16. "Personal Impressions of a Candidate"; "The Battle Is Over."
17. "The Battle Is Over."
18. "Former Mayor J. M. Earp Is Dead."
19. "The Case of Mr. Earp"; "The City Campaign Gets Warmer."
20. "More of Mr. Earp's Reasons."
21. "The Case of Mr. Earp"; "Earp Is the Next Mayor."
22. "Lamar Has a Chamber of Commerce"; "Rain Can't Daunt Members of New C of C"; "Name C of C Committees."
23. "Will George Save Us From Soup?"; "Ninety Banqueters Attend."
24. "Sell Your Hammer and Buy a Horn."
25. "Chamber of Commerce"; "Want to Back Off on the Bond Election"; "Wants to Pave the Square."
26. White interview by author, July 6, 1992; "Talk About Paving the Square"; "Council Stands Unanimous for Paving the Square"; "Oiling the Streets."
27. Luanna Aull, "A Tribute to a Wonderful Man"; "Talk About Paving the Square."
28. "Council Stands Unanimous for Paving the Square"; "The Remon-

strance Against Paving Could Not Muster Majority"; "Council Now Free to Proceed With Paving"; "Contract Let for Paving Lamar Square."

29. "Saturday the First Day All of the Square Was Open."

30. "Second White Way for Square."

31. "Would Oust Lake Cemetery Association"; "Breaks Up in a Big Row."

32. "Breaks Up in a Big Row."

33. "Made It Easy to Get In"; "$60,000 Cemetery Endowment."

34. "They Talked About the Hospital."

35. "An Eleven to One Victory for the Hospital."

36. "What We Can Do to Help Lamar."

37. *Official Manual of the State of Missouri for the Years 1935–1936,* 854; Richard S. Kirkendall, *A History of Missouri, Volume V, 1919 to 1953,* 162; "The Traveling Brain Trusters Are Making Relief Impossible."

38. "The Traveling Brain Trusters Are Making Relief Impossible"; "Resigns Relief Post in Ire at 'Brain Trust.'"

39. "The Traveling Brain Trusters"; "Resignation Not Accepted."

CHAPTER 7

1. Luanna Aull, "Obstacles? Not Many!"

2. White interview by author, July 6, 1992; Eddy, "Ripsnorting News," 136.

3. Madeleine Aull Van Hafften, "Gleanings," July 25, 1964.

4. *Lamar Democrat,* January 16, 1908.

5. Luanna Aull, "Gleanings," September 29, 1953; Luanna Aull, "A Tribute to a Wonderful Man."

6. Luanna Aull, "Filling Space."

7. Luanna Aull, "Today's Poem," November 10, 1955; Luanna Aull, "Today's Poem," October 9, 1958.

8. Luanna Aull, "Gleanings," November 16, 1963.

9. Luanna Aull, "Gleanings," January 5, 1963; Young, *Down Memory Lane,* 70; *Lamar Democrat,* January 11, 1906.

10. Luanna Aull, "Gleanings," February 20, 1964; White interview by author, July 6, 1992.

11. White interview by author, March 16, 1994; "The Panhandler Is Back"; "Ed Didn't Have to Go to Jail."

12. Luanna Aull, "Gleanings," April 28, 1955.

13. White interview by author, March 16, 1994.

14. "Nell Casement dies."

15. "Thirty Years with the Democrat."

16. Luanna Aull, "Gleanings," June 2, 1960; Luanna Aull, "All for Naught"; Luanna Aull, "Gleanings," December 27, 1956.

17. *Lamar Democrat,* September 20, 1923; Luanna Aull, "Gleanings," May 25, 1963; Luanna Aull, "Gleanings," September 27, 1962.

18. Luanna Aull, "Keep Cool!"

19. Madeleine Aull Van Hafften, "Gleanings," November 13, 1965; Luanna Aull, "Gleanings," August 18, 1955.

20. Luanna Aull, "Destination vs. Destitution."

21. Margaret Hamilton, "Aull's Daughter Becomes Editor Without Studying Journalism."

22. White interview by author, March 16, 1994.

23. Randy Turner, "Longtime Democrat co-publisher is dead."

24. "Tige McDaniel Killed, Betty Aull Painfully Hurt."

25. White interview by author, March 16, 1994.

26. Ibid.

27. Ibid.

28. *Lamar Democrat,* September 9, 1941.

29. *Lamar Democrat,* December 26, 1941.

30. Carl Van Hafften, "From Rags to Riches"; "A Great Dither About the Dogs"; "It Was Lonesome Without the Dogs"; "Day of Deliverance for the Dogs."

31. "The End for Tippy."

CHAPTER 8

1. "Democrat Editor Has Sudden Development of Eye Trouble."

2. "The Old Yellow Buggy Comes Back to the Square"; Hamilton, "Aull's Daughter Becomes Editor."

3. Hamilton, "Aull's Daughter Becomes Editor."

4. "Arthur Aull to Mayo's"; "Back from Mayo's."

5. "A Little Note to My Friends"; Hamilton, "Aull's Daughter Becomes Editor."

6. "A Note from the Boss."

7. Eddy, "Ripsnorting News," 136; "Arthur Aull"; "Left No Will."

8. "Last Rites Held for Arthur Aull at Lamar Today."

9. "The Eulogy on Arthur Aull."

10. "A Contrast."

11. "A Great Editor Is Dead"; "Editor Arthur Aull's Pen Has Now Run Dry."

12. "Editor Dies."

13. "Announcement By Publisher."

14. "The Lamar Daily Journal Sold." The *Lamar Leader,* a weekly, ceased publication in May 1952. The *Lamar Republican* changed its name to the *Lamar Journal* in 1950.

15. "Divorce Suit"; Madeleine Aull Van Hafften, "Gleanings," May 9, 1965.

16. "Mrs. Arthur Aull Dead"; Chad Stebbins, "A Biography of James C. Kirkpatrick," 77.

17. Warden, "All the News That's Fit to Print."

18. The Missouri Newspaper Hall of Fame was established by the Missouri Press Association in 1991. Inductees include Joseph Charless, who established the state's first newspaper in 1808; Joseph Pulitzer, founder of the *St. Louis Post-Dispatch;* Walter Williams, founding dean of the University of Missouri School of Journalism; William Rockhill Nelson, founder of the *Kansas City Star;* and Mark Twain, who began his newspaper career in Hannibal, Mo.

19. *Lamar Democrat,* January 30, 1908.

20. Blaise, "Irrepressible Country Editor."

21. White interview by author, July 6, 1992.

22. "Arthur Aull Dies; Editor in Missouri"; Eddy, "Ripsnorting News," 134; Blaise, "Irrepressible Country Editor."

23. "Pepper and Salt," July 14, 1944.

24. "What's the Matter with the Farm?"; "What's the Matter?"; "What's the Matter with the Courts?"

25. White interview by author, March 16, 1994; Luanna Aull, "A Tribute to a Wonderful Man," 2.

26. Carol Lynn Gilmer, "Missouri's One-Family Newspaper," 52; "First Installment of Digest Poll Next Week Pretty Sure to Favor Landon"; *Lamar Democrat,* May 7, 1935; "Here Goes Our Prediction for 1941, Before the End of the Year America Will Be Forced to Enter the War."

27. *Lamar Democrat,* August 29, 1918; "How Hoover Became President, and Why He's Likely to Stay President for Some Time"; "We Told You So! We Told You So!!" 6.

BIBLIOGRAPHICAL ESSAY

All the News Is Fit to Print: Profile of a Country Editor can be written only because Arthur Aull's newspaper, the *Lamar Democrat,* has been preserved on microfilm by the State Historical Society of Missouri. The Society possesses nearly a continuous run of the weekly *Democrat* from May 1883 to October 1929, when Aull converted the paper to semiweekly publication. The Society has every issue of Aull's semiweekly *Democrat.*

But because Aull's *Daily Democrat* does not exist in the Society's archives or anywhere else, a study of his editorship is limited in its reach. Although Aull included his most sensational stories in the weekly and semiweekly editions, it is not clear whether the content of these papers is representative of his daily. The demise of the *Daily Democrat* also makes it difficult to track Aull's news coverage of certain issues and substantiate the three threats on his life that Betty Aull White described. Nevertheless, the thirty-two hundred existing issues of the weekly and semiweekly paper constitute a rich historical resource. They are the primary means to reconstruct the forty-eight years of Aull's *Democrat,* because none of the paper's business records or correspondence was preserved.

Although newspapers are a rich source of historical evidence, their credibility and accuracy must always be checked. For example, Aull's obituary in the *Democrat* listed the date of his wedding as March 2, 1896; his wife's obituary stated it was March 9, 1896. An examination of Barton County marriage records, however, revealed the actual date to be March 22, 1896. Valuable secondary material came from the many articles written about Aull in the national media, but in some cases its validity was suspect, too. The *New York Times,* for example, reported in its obituary of Aull that he was "perhaps the last of that frontier breed of editors who kept a revolver handy." But according to Aull's daughter Betty, he never handled a gun in his life.

A handy secondary source was Marvin L. VanGilder's *The Story of Barton County,* published in 1972, although the dates for Aull's marriage and the birth of his first daughter, Madeleine, were incorrect. *The Story of Barton County* provided a good account of the history of Barton County, and its biographical sketches of many of Lamar's leading citizens were particularly helpful. Other historical resources used included county records, city directories, and the tombstones of Lake Cemetery in Lamar and Oakton Cemetery. Sally Foreman Griffith's *Home Town News: William Allen White and the Emporia Gazette* and Calder Pickett's *Ed Howe: Country Town Philosopher* were frequently consulted as good examples of biographies of country newspaper editors.

Aside from what appears in his obituary in the *Democrat* and a retrospective piece his wife wrote in 1957, little is known about Aull's pre-*Democrat* days. He wrote no memoirs, kept no diary or journal, and did not reminisce about his life in the paper. Some information about his childhood did come from his father's 1930 obituary in the *Democrat.* Luanna Aull's "Gleanings" columns in the *Democrat* after her husband's death provided much of the material for chapter 7, "Family Man."

Chapter 2, "Newspaper War," was limited by the fact that Lamar's *Industrial Leader* is available from only July 7, 1901, to November 6, 1901 (the *Industrial Leader* was the weekly version of the daily *Lamar Leader,* of which only a few scattered issues are preserved). Although Aull's nasty newspaper war with Arthur Rozelle, publisher of the *Leader,* fell during this four-month period of 1901, their criminal libel trial occurred in January 1902. The *Leader's* perspective on the bitter trial is not available, except for a paragraph reprinted in the *Golden City Free Press,* another newspaper in Barton County. The *Lamar Republican,* another participant in the newspaper war, is available on microfilm from August 8, 1901, to September 18, 1902.

Microfilm of the *Lamar Republican-Sentinel* exists from November 28, 1907, to June 10, 1920, and was useful in chapter 4, "A Lynching in Lamar." Aull reprinted an editorial from a neighboring paper, the *Oskaloosa News,* that assailed the newspapers of Lamar for their failure to denounce the mob action of May 28, 1919. The *Oskaloosa News* no longer exists, but because the *Republican-Sentinel* also reprinted the editorial, it was possible to compare the two versions.

Still another source was a family scrapbook spanning the years 1936 to 1972. Nell Casement, the longtime office manager of the *Democrat,* saved all the articles written about Aull and many of the letters he and daughter Madeleine Aull Van Hafften received from throughout the country. Adlai E. Stevenson, for example, wrote to Van Hafften on December 9, 1952, thanking her for supporting his presidential campaign.

The Aull family limits access to the scrapbook, which in 1992 was in the possession of a granddaughter, Luanna Noyes Martin, of Springfield, Missouri. This researcher was allowed to make notes from the scrapbook one afternoon and select a few articles and letters to be copied at a commercial printing service. Most valuable of the articles was a commentary by the publisher of the *Lamar Republican* upon Aull's death in 1948. The *Lamar Republican* of the 1940s is not available on microfilm.

BIBLIOGRAPHY

ARTICLES

"All the News." *Time,* July 8, 1946, 52.

"Announcement By Publisher." *Lamar Democrat,* September 29, 1953.

"Arthur Aull." *Carthage Evening Press,* May 10, 1948.

"Arthur Aull Dies; Editor in Missouri." *New York Times,* May 9, 1948.

"Arthur Aull Funeral Tomorrow; Editor Who Pulled No Punches." *St. Louis Post-Dispatch,* May 9, 1948.

"Arthur Aull Natureman." *Lamar Democrat,* August 24, 1911.

"Arthur Aull to Mayo's." *Lamar Democrat,* October 8, 1946.

"Arthur Rozelle Near Death." *Lamar Democrat,* June 27, 1912.

"As to Mr. Moore's Note." *Lamar Democrat,* November 12, 1908.

"As to Mr. Moore's Reply." *Lamar Democrat,* November 19, 1908.

"As to Punishing the Mob." *Lamar Democrat,* June 5, 1919.

"The Attitude of the Democrat." *Lamar Democrat,* September 10, 1908.

Aull, Luanna. "All for Naught." *Lamar Democrat,* September 1, 1953.

———. "Arthur Gets Posies." *Lamar Democrat,* February 14, 1941.

———. "Destination vs. Destitution." *Lamar Democrat,* April 14, 1955.

———. "Filling Space." *Lamar Democrat,* May 19, 1955.

———. "Gleanings." *Lamar Democrat,* September 29, 1953.

———. "Gleanings." *Lamar Democrat,* April 28, 1955.

———. "Gleanings." *Lamar Democrat,* August 18, 1955.

———. "Gleanings." *Lamar Democrat,* December 27, 1956.

———. "Gleanings." *Lamar Democrat,* February 7, 1957.

———. "Gleanings." *Lamar Democrat,* February 20, 1958.

———. "Gleanings." *Lamar Democrat,* November 19, 1959.

———. "Gleanings." *Lamar Democrat,* June 2, 1960.

———. "Gleanings." *Lamar Democrat,* July 21, 1960.

————. "Gleanings." *Lamar Democrat,* September 14, 1961.

————. "Gleanings." *Lamar Democrat,* September 27, 1962.

————. "Gleanings." *Lamar Democrat,* January 5, 1963.

————. "Gleanings." *Lamar Democrat,* May 25, 1963.

————. "Gleanings." *Lamar Democrat,* June 8, 1963.

————. "Gleanings." *Lamar Democrat,* November 16, 1963.

————. "Gleanings." *Lamar Democrat,* February 20, 1964.

————. "Keep Cool!" *Lamar Democrat,* November 10, 1953.

————. "Obstacles? Not Many!" *Lamar Democrat,* March 24, 1953.

————. "Today's Poem." *Lamar Democrat,* November 10, 1955.

————. "Today's Poem." *Lamar Democrat,* October 9, 1958.

————. "A Tribute to a Wonderful Man." *Lamar Democrat,* September 6, 1957.

————. "A Word to the Voters." *Lamar Democrat,* March 30, 1961.

"Back from Mayo's." *Lamar Democrat,* October 18, 1946.

"Back Wash on the Lynch Hanging," *Lamar Democrat,* June 19, 1919.

"The Battle Is Over." *Lamar Democrat,* April 8, 1920.

"Biography and Comments on the Death of William Aull," *Lamar Democrat,* June 24, 1930.

"Birds of a Feather." *Lamar Industrial Leader,* August 23, 1901.

Blaise, H. V. "Irrepressible Country Editor." *St. Louis Post-Dispatch,* June 30, 1946.

"Bolshevism in Missouri." *Kansas City Post,* May 29, 1919.

"The Boss Says Flying in a Liner is Kinda Dull—But He Likes It That Way." *Lamar Democrat,* February 18, 1941.

"A Boy Burglar." *Lamar Democrat,* July 28, 1904.

"The Boys in Lamar Are Drinking Real Beer." *Lamar Democrat,* April 11, 1933.

"A Bran New Paper This Week." *Lamar Democrat,* October 1, 1929.

"Breaks Up in a Big Row." *Lamar Democrat,* January 6, 1921.

"By Her Own Hand." *Lamar Democrat,* July 16, 1908.

"By the Skin of His Teeth." *Lamar Democrat,* April 8, 1920.

"Career of John M. Harlow." *Lamar Democrat,* March 13, 1919.

"The Case of a Good Man Enthralled by Liquor." *Lamar Democrat,* November 5, 1935.

"The Case of Mr. Earp." *Lamar Democrat,* April 7, 1921.

"Caught a Tigress." *Lamar Democrat,* May 19, 1904.

Cauley, John R. "Aull Prints All the News." *Life,* February 26, 1945, 8, 10.

"Chamber of Commerce." *Lamar Democrat,* January 1, 1920.

"Charged With Attempted Rape of Three Year Old Girl." *Lamar Democrat,* September 13, 1946.
"Charged With Libel." *Lamar Industrial Leader,* September 20, 1901.
"Charlie Slates Convicted of Illicit Relationships with Girl 10!" *Lamar Democrat,* September 18, 1942.
"Chas B. Whalen Is Released." *Lamar Democrat,* May 24, 1940.
"The City Campaign Gets Warmer." *Lamar Democrat,* April 7, 1921.
"Clear Case of Robbery." *Lamar Industrial Leader,* July 26, 1901.
"The Coal Fields Are Declining." *Lamar Democrat,* June 8, 1911.
"Come Quick." *Lamar Democrat,* December 10, 1908.
"Come to Blows." *Lamar Democrat,* October 8, 1903.
"The Comment of President Truman." *Lamar Democrat,* May 14, 1948.
"The Committee's Report." *Lamar Industrial Leader,* August 16, 1901.
"Completes Lynch's Criminal Record." *Lamar Democrat,* March 20, 1919.
"Contract Let for Paving Lamar Square." *Lamar Democrat,* July 22, 1926.
"A Contrast." *Lamar Democrat,* May 14, 1948.
"Cook's Evening Out." *Missouri Press News,* November 1938, 5–11.
"Council Now Free to Proceed With Paving." *Lamar Democrat,* June 10, 1926.
"Council Stands Unanimous for Paving the Square." *Lamar Democrat,* May 20, 1926.
"Country Editor." *Chicago Daily News,* October 23, 1943.
"A Country Editor Who Knows His Readers Want Life 'As Is.' " *Kansas City Star,* June 6, 1937.
"Court Grants Nine Divorces." *Lamar Democrat,* September 15, 1927.
"Criminal Record of Man Hanged by Mob at Lamar." *St. Louis Star,* May 29, 1919.
"The Day for Divorces." *Lamar Democrat,* September 19, 1912.
"Day of Deliverance for the Dogs." *Lamar Democrat,* July 7, 1944.
"Death Penalty for Six Crimes." *Lamar Democrat,* July 10, 1919.
"Democrat Editor Has Sudden Development of Eye Trouble." *Lamar Democrat,* August 25, 1942.
"The Democrat Will Move." *Lamar Democrat,* January 28, 1909.
"Democrats and Libel." *Golden City Free Press,* January 30, 1902.
"Died at St. John's Hospital." *Lamar Democrat,* March 13, 1919.
"Divorce Suit." *Lamar Democrat,* October 5, 1951.
"Does It Love Them!" *Lamar Democrat,* July 18, 1901.
"Don't Shoot the Fiddler, He's Doing His Best." *Lamar Democrat,* April 8, 1938.

"Dorothy Sullivan Tells Her Story, Whallen Tells His." *Lamar Democrat,* February 9, 1940.

"Dorothy Sullivan Told a Story Such As Was Never Before Told in a Barton County Court." *Lamar Democrat,* January 9, 1940.

"Dr. Montgomery Was Arrested." *Lamar Democrat,* September 15, 1921.

"Earp Is the Next Mayor." *Lamar Democrat,* April 7, 1921.

"Ed Didn't Have to Go to Jail." *Lamar Democrat,* May 3, 1928.

Eddy, Don. "Ripsnorting News." *American Magazine,* June 1949, 134–37.

"Editor Arthur Aull's Pen Has Now Run Dry." *Liberal News,* May 14, 1948.

"Editor Dies." *Lamar Republican,* May 10, 1948.

"An Eight Year Old Mail Robber." *Lamar Democrat,* July 22, 1920.

"An Eleven to One Victory for the Hospital." *Lamar Democrat,* February 22, 1946.

"The End for Familiar Lamar Character." *Lamar Democrat,* July 9, 1959.

"The End for Tippy." *Lamar Democrat,* September 17, 1946.

"The End of 'Lamar's Great Store.'" *Lamar Democrat,* December 6, 1928.

"The Eulogy on Arthur Aull." *Lamar Democrat,* May 14, 1948.

"A Fake 'Letter.'" *Lamar Democrat,* August 22, 1901.

"Farewell, a Long Farewell." *Lamar Democrat,* April 8, 1909.

"First Installment of Digest Poll Next Week Pretty Sure to Favor Landon." *Lamar Democrat,* August 28, 1936.

"Five Hundred Dollars in Gold." *Lamar Democrat,* May 4, 1911.

"Former Mayor J. M. Earp Is Dead." *Lamar Democrat,* June 23, 1939.

"Four Couples Granted Freedom." *Lamar Democrat,* April 18, 1912.

"Four Quit, Two Go Together." *Lamar Democrat,* April 20, 1911.

"Friends Bid Farewell to Hon. E. L. Moore." *Lamar Democrat,* August 25, 1942.

"From the Lamar Democrat 25 Years Ago." *Lamar Democrat,* October 10, 1941.

"Gardner Signs Bill Restoring Death Penalty." *St. Louis Republic,* July 9, 1919.

Gilmer, Carol Lynn. "Missouri's One-Family Newspaper." *Harper's Magazine,* October 1954, 52–57.

"Got Eddie's Baby's Age Wrong. For Such Awful Lie He's Sure We Have to Take Sleeping Powder." *Lamar Democrat,* February 25, 1941.

"Governor Asks Information." *St. Louis Daily Globe-Democrat,* May 30, 1919.

"Governor Offers Prosecutor Aid in Lynch Hanging." *St. Louis Post-Dispatch,* May 30, 1919.

"A Great Dither About the Dogs." *Lamar Democrat,* May 19, 1944.

"A Great Editor Is Dead." *Golden City Herald,* May 13, 1948.

"Grim and Grisly." *Lamar Democrat,* July 31, 1902.

"The Growth of the Lamar Post Office." *Lamar Democrat,* January 10, 1924.

Hamilton, Margaret. "Aull's Daughter Becomes Editor Without Studying Journalism." *Kansas City Star,* November 24, 1946.

Harger, Charles Moreau. "The Country Editor of To-Day." *Atlantic Monthly,* January 1907, 89–96.

"Has Been Tough on the Misses." *Lamar Democrat,* April 15, 1938.

"He Says Hurrah for Lamar." *Lamar Democrat,* June 5, 1919.

"He Shaved the President." *Lamar Democrat,* July 17, 1902.

"Here Goes Our Prediction for 1941, Before the End of the Year America Will Be Forced to Enter the War." *Lamar Democrat,* January 10, 1941.

"Here's the Story." *Lamar Democrat,* February 18, 1941.

"Here's What They Say." *Lamar Democrat,* December 17, 1914.

"History of the Piano Case." *Lamar Democrat,* April 14, 1910.

"Hot Klan Battle at Liberal." *Lamar Democrat,* April 3, 1924.

House, Jay E. "The Old Country Weekly." *Saturday Evening Post,* May 12, 1934, 25, 52.

"How Hoover Became President, and Why He's Likely to Stay President for Some Time." *Lamar Democrat,* November 22, 1928.

"How Would the Readers Answer This Question?" *Lamar Democrat,* July 28, 1927.

"In Relation to the Lamar Public Schools." *Lamar Democrat,* March 29, 1917.

"Inquest Develops the Evidence." *Lamar Democrat,* March 13, 1919.

"Investigation Demanded." *Lamar Industrial Leader,* August 23, 1901.

"It Was Divorce Day." *Lamar Democrat,* September 22, 1910.

"It Was Lonesome Without the Dogs." *Lamar Democrat,* May 23, 1944.

"Jar of Stones Came From Patient's Gall Cyst." *Lamar Democrat,* July 28, 1933.

"Jay Lynch Gets Life Sentence." *Lamar Republican-Sentinel,* May 29, 1919.

"Jury Acquitted Whallen." *Lamar Democrat,* February 9, 1940.

"Jury Could Learn Nothing About Lynching." *Lamar Democrat,* September 11, 1919.

"A Klan Is Forming in Lamar." *Lamar Democrat,* July 6, 1922.

"Klan Issues Its Paper at Mulberry." *Lamar Democrat,* September 23, 1923.

"Klan to Make Demonstration in Lamar." *Lamar Democrat,* December 6, 1923.

"Lamar Case Dismissed." *Lamar Democrat,* February 5, 1935.

"The Lamar Daily Journal Sold." *Lamar Democrat,* September 13, 1954.

"Lamar Has a Chamber of Commerce." *Lamar Democrat,* October 23, 1919.

"Lamar Has Her First Ku Klux Parade." *Lamar Democrat,* June 12, 1924.

"Lamar Loses Her Premier Lawyer and Citizen." *Lamar Democrat,* August 25, 1942.

"The Lamar Lynching." *St. Louis Post-Dispatch,* May 29, 1919.

"Last Rites Held for Arthur Aull at Lamar Today." *Carthage Evening Press,* May 10, 1948.

"The Leader Contest Closes." *Lamar Democrat,* August 10, 1911.

"Left No Will." *Lamar Democrat,* May 14, 1948.

"The Libel Cases." *Lamar Republican,* January 30, 1902.

"A Little Note to My Friends." *Lamar Democrat,* November 5, 1946.

"Lynch Brought to Lamar." *Lamar Democrat,* May 29, 1919.

"Lynch Faced Five Year Term." *Lamar Democrat,* March 6, 1919.

"Lynch Hanged to an Elm Tree." *Lamar Democrat,* May 29, 1919.

"Lynch is in the Butler Jail." *Lamar Democrat,* May 22, 1919.

"Lynch Persisted in Staying to See His Wife." *Lamar Democrat,* June 5, 1919.

"Lynch Trial Postponed." *Lamar Democrat,* November 27, 1919.

"Lynch's Body at Forest Park Cemetery." *Lamar Democrat,* June 5, 1919.

"Mable Mott Marries Kewpie Kewps." *Lamar Democrat,* June 8, 1922.

"Made It Easy to Get In." *Lamar Democrat,* January 13, 1921.

"Many Women in Mob that Hanged Slayer of Sheriff Harlow." *St. Louis Daily Globe-Democrat,* May 30, 1919.

"Mark Sure Wants It Stopped." *Lamar Democrat,* December 22, 1910.

"Martha Lamar Mother of Rex Sues Paper for Fifty Thousand." *Lamar Democrat,* November 30, 1934.

"Merchants and Business Men Bring Christmas Greetings." *Lamar Democrat,* December 19, 1944.

"A Mighty Cheap Press, Folder, Chases and Motor for Some Country Paper." *Lamar Democrat,* August 29, 1929.

"Milestones." *Time,* May 17, 1948, 99.

"Miss Adams Wins." *Lamar Democrat,* December 29, 1910.

"Miss Bartlett Awarded the Piano." *Lamar Democrat,* January 6, 1910.

"Miss Davidson Is Not Married." *Lamar Democrat,* June 12, 1919.

"Miss Isenhower Wins." *Lamar Democrat,* October 5, 1911.

"Miss Mae Hylton Under Surgeon's Knife." *Lamar Democrat,* September 3, 1940.

"Missouri Editor, 'Fiery and Outspoken,' Has Made His Paper Known All Over U.S." *Publishers' Auxiliary,* September 11, 1937, 7.

"Mr. Moore's Reply." *Lamar Democrat,* November 12, 1908.

"Mob Enters Court and Hangs a Life Convict Sentenced Under Law Barring Death Penalty." *New York Times,* May 29, 1919.

"A Mob Hangs Lynch at 3:45." *Lamar Republican-Sentinel,* May 29, 1919.

"Mob Hangs Slayer." *Kansas City Times,* May 29, 1919.

"Monday Was Divorce Day." *Lamar Democrat,* April 14, 1921.

"More of Mr. Earp's Reasons." *Lamar Democrat,* April 7, 1921.

"The Most Horrible Wreck That Ever Occurred in Barton County." *Lamar Democrat,* September 7, 1943.

"Mr. Rozelle Dead." *Lamar Democrat,* July 4, 1912.

"Mrs. Arthur Aull Dead." *Lamar Democrat,* April 18, 1968.

"Mrs. Brooks Passionately Denies Circulating the Petition." *Lamar Democrat,* June 4, 1943.

"Mrs. Jackson Gets Into Our Wool." *Lamar Democrat,* June 9, 1921.

"Mrs. Maude Lynch Acquitted." *Lamar Democrat,* July 1, 1920.

"Much Discussion of the Whallen Sodomy Case." *Lamar Democrat,* February 13, 1940.

"Name C of C Committees." *Lamar Democrat,* November 6, 1919.

"Nell Casement Dies." *Lamar Democrat,* May 15, 1973.

"Ninety Banqueters Attend." *Lamar Democrat,* November 27, 1919.

"No Lynchers Ever Tried?" *Kansas City Star,* May 29, 1919.

"No Opposition." *Lamar Democrat,* April 5, 1917.

"No Relief." *Golden City Free Press,* July 26, 1901.

"A Note from the Boss." *Lamar Democrat,* April 1, 1947.

"Oiling the Streets." *Lamar Democrat,* March 22, 1917.

"The Old Yellow Buggy Comes Back to the Square." *Lamar Democrat,* September 11, 1942.

"Oliver P. Turnbull." *Lamar Democrat,* March 1, 1923.

"1000 Hear About the Ku Klux Klan." *Lamar Democrat,* July 13, 1922.

"Out of Ten Divorces, Nine Go to Women." *Lamar Democrat,* September 12, 1941.

"Owens Had Long Criminal Record." *Lamar Democrat,* March 13, 1919.

"The Panhandler Is Back." *Lamar Democrat,* December 22, 1921.

"Paper Lost on the Gold Awards." *Lamar Democrat,* January 15, 1925.

"Pay!" *Lamar Democrat,* December 6, 1900.

"Pay." *Lamar Democrat,* December 11, 1902.

"Pepper and Salt." *Lamar Democrat,* December 3, 1940.

"Pepper and Salt." *Lamar Democrat,* July 14, 1944.

"Pepper and Salt." *Lamar Democrat,* May 1, 1945.

"Personal Impressions of a Candidate." *Lamar Democrat,* April 8, 1920.

"Petition Presented to the Paper Asking That It Forbid the Mention of Beer, Whiskey and Other Alcoholic Drinks in the Advertisements." *Lamar Democrat,* January 10, 1936.

"The Piano into Court." *Lamar Democrat,* January 20, 1910.

"A 'Pie' Combination." *Lamar Democrat,* July 25, 1901.

"Prosecutor Has Names of 9 Men in Lynch Mob." *St. Louis Post-Dispatch,* May 29, 1919.

"Put Up or Shut Up." *Lamar Industrial Leader,* August 23, 1901.

"Rain Can't Daunt Members of New C of C." *Lamar Democrat,* October 30, 1919.

"A Really Startling Divorce Petition." *Lamar Democrat,* October 6, 1927.

"The Remonstrance Against Paving Could Not Muster Majority." *Lamar Democrat,* June 10, 1926.

"Resignation Not Accepted." *Lamar Democrat,* February 26, 1935.

"Resigns Relief Post in Ire at 'Brain Trust.'" *New York Times,* February 22, 1935.

"Result of the Investigation." *Lamar Democrat,* August 15, 1901.

"Rev. Jones Is for the Klan." *Lamar Democrat,* June 22, 1922.

"Rev. Ward Brings Us an Article from Zions Herald Declaring That Japan is Breaking." *Lamar Democrat,* July 28, 1938.

"Rev. Ward Feels That We Misrepresented the Pacifists and Are Unfair to Them." *Lamar Democrat,* July 1, 1938.

"Rev. Ward Takes Yours Truly to the Woodshed." *Lamar Democrat,* May 19, 1936.

"Romantic and Marvelous Story of Lynch's Escape." *Lamar Democrat,* May 22, 1919.

"The Root of Lynching." *St. Louis Star,* May 29, 1919.

Rose, Will. "The Small-Town Newspaper Divorces Its Party." *Scribner's Magazine,* March 1926, 314–15.

"Round and Round Over Klan Meeting." *Lamar Democrat,* February 8, 1923.

"Saturday the First Day All of the Square Was Open." *Lamar Democrat,* December 9, 1926.

"Saved Women From Mob." *Kansas City Star,* May 29, 1919.

"Says Good Bye to School Board." *Lamar Democrat,* March 29, 1923.

"Scorns a Cussin' Editor." *Kansas City Times,* May 20, 1936.

"Second White Way for Square." *Lamar Democrat,* April 18, 1929.

"Seek Evidence on Mob." *Kansas City Times,* May 30, 1919.

"Sell Your Hammer and Buy a Horn." *Lamar Democrat,* December 25, 1919.

"Several Men Freed from Matrimony." *Lamar Democrat,* September 12, 1918.

"Sharps and Flats." *Boonville Weekly Advertiser,* September 20, 1901.

"Sharps and Flats." *Boonville Weekly Advertiser,* October 4, 1901.

"She Wanted a Divorce, and She Wanted It Bad." *Lamar Democrat,* March 11, 1909.

"Sheriff Harlow Sleeps Among Old Neighbors." *Lamar Democrat,* March 6, 1919.

"Sheriff J. M. Harlow Murdered." *Lamar Democrat,* March 6, 1919.

"Sheriff Recognized Leaders of Mob that Hanged Jay Lynch." *St. Louis Post-Dispatch,* May 29, 1919.

"$60,000 Cemetery Endowment." *Lamar Democrat,* March 31, 1921.

"Some Country Papers on the Lynch Hanging." *Lamar Democrat,* June 12, 1919.

"Some Plain Talk." *Lamar Democrat,* November 5, 1908.

"Speaking the Public Mind." *Lamar Democrat,* July 10, 1934.

"Splattered Brains and Blood All Over His Three Children." *Lamar Democrat,* February 14, 1939.

"Statement of the Ownership, Management, Circulation, Etc., Required by the Act of Congress of August 24, 1912." *Lamar Democrat,* March 28, 1918.

"Still More Want Divorces." *Lamar Democrat,* September 6, 1923.

"Still Talk About Lynch." *Lamar Democrat,* June 5, 1919.

"State vs. Arthur Aull." *Lamar Democrat,* January 30, 1902.

"Statement in Regard to the Schoolboard." *Lamar Democrat,* April 1, 1920.

"Story of a Great Store." *Lamar Democrat,* October 10, 1912.

"The Story of Lamar's First Lynching Just Forty Years Ago." *Lamar Democrat,* January 29, 1932.

"Story of West Barton Coal Field, Now Practically Dug Out, Reads Like a Legend of Gold." *Lamar Democrat,* March 29, 1938.

"Talk About Paving the Square." *Lamar Democrat,* February 15, 1923.

"Talks Right Out Loud." *Lamar Republican-Sentinel,* June 19, 1919.

"Tear Gas Bomb at Ku Klux Meeting." *Lamar Democrat,* July 3, 1924.

"Tells the Governor Where to Begin in Lynch Case." *Lamar Democrat,* June 5, 1919.

"Ten Divorces Granted, Monday." *Lamar Democrat,* September 13, 1935.

"Ten Thousand Dollar Suit Against Lamar Democrat Dismissed by Judge Hendricks." *Lamar Democrat,* April 14, 1931.

"A Ten Year Old Burglar." *Lamar Democrat,* September 2, 1926.

"Terrific Fight in Barber Shop." *Lamar Democrat,* November 8, 1917.

"They Heard the White Robed Klansman." *Lamar Democrat,* December 13, 1923.

"They Talked About the Hospital." *Lamar Democrat,* September 25, 1945.

"They Tell Their Marital Woes." *Lamar Democrat,* September 23, 1915.

"Thirteen Brief Stories of Ruined Marriages," *Lamar Democrat,* September 13, 1940.

"Thirteen Year Old Boy Dead Drunk." *Lamar Democrat,* February 20, 1940.

"Thirty Years with the Democrat." *Lamar Democrat,* May 26, 1955.

"Threatened to Lynch the Women." *Lamar Democrat,* June 5, 1919.

"Tige McDaniel Killed, Betty Aull Painfully Hurt." *Lamar Democrat,* January 5, 1932.

"Tiny Is Sour on Lamar." *Lamar Democrat,* September 8, 1944.

"To a Dollar and a Half a Year." *Lamar Democrat,* November 21, 1918.

"To Go to Hell vs. Don't Give a Damn." *Lamar Democrat,* November 28, 1912.

"To Investigate Lynch Hanging." *Lamar Democrat,* September 11, 1919.

"To Our Readers." *Lamar Democrat,* January 16, 1908.

"To the People of Barton County." *Lamar Democrat,* August 9, 1900.

"Toss Harkless Is Dead!" *Lamar Democrat,* April 1, 1932.

"The Tragedies of Love." *Lamar Democrat,* September 18, 1919.

"The Tragedies That Follow the Altar." *Lamar Democrat,* September 23, 1920.

"Transition." *Newsweek,* May 17, 1948, 70.

"The Traveling Brain Trusters Are Making Relief Impossible." *Lamar Democrat,* February 22, 1935.

"Tries to Get the Facts." *Lamar Republican-Sentinel,* June 12, 1919.

"Truman Day a Wonderful Day." *Lamar Democrat,* September 1, 1944.

"Truman Makes His Address to Ten Thousand." *Lamar Democrat,* September 5, 1944.

Turner, Randy. "Longtime Democrat co-publisher is dead." *Lamar Democrat,* July 20, 1989.

"Two Distinguished Newspapermen from Chicago Spent Two Days in Lamar." *Lamar Democrat,* October 12, 1943.

"Under an Ozark Moon." *Newsweek,* September 11, 1944, 39–40.

"Unseen Committee Issues Statement." *Lamar Democrat,* April 8, 1920.

"Up to Rozelle." *Lamar Democrat,* August 22, 1901.

Van Hafften, Carl. "From Rags to Riches." *Lamar Democrat,* September 17, 1946.

Van Hafften, Madeleine Aull. "Arthur Aull Is Dead." *Lamar Democrat,* May 11, 1948.

———. "Gleanings." *Lamar Democrat,* July 25, 1964.

———. "Gleanings." *Lamar Democrat,* May 9, 1965.

———. "Gleanings." *Lamar Democrat,* November 13, 1965.

———. "A Middle Westerner on the Sidewalks of New York." *Lamar Democrat,* February 28, 1941.

"Verdict of Acquittal." *Lamar Democrat,* January 30, 1902.

"A Visitor Brings Us Back to Auld Lang Syne." *Lamar Democrat,* June 2, 1942.

"Walter Kremp Sues The Democrat for Ten Thousand Dollars." *Lamar Democrat,* October 7, 1930.

"Want to Back Off on the Bond Election." *Lamar Democrat,* January 8, 1920.

"Wants to Pave the Square." *Lamar Democrat,* January 29, 1920.

Warden, Rob. "All the News That's Fit to Print (And a Little Something Extra) Down in Lamar, Missouri." *Chicago Daily News,* December 23–24, 1972.

"Warrants May Be Issued in Lamar Hanging." *St. Louis Star,* May 29, 1919.

"Watching Two Men Die." *Lamar Democrat,* August 9, 1923.

"We Certainly got One Bloody Head at the Eversall House." *Lamar Democrat,* August 10, 1943.

"We Get Another Write-Up." *Lamar Democrat,* September 15, 1944.

"We Pulled a Good One." *Lamar Democrat,* January 23, 1919.

"We Told You So! We Told You So!!" *Lamar Democrat,* September 20, 1938.

"Well, We Say Too, What About These Warrants." *Lamar Democrat,* October 19, 1934.

"Whalen Convicted, But Jury Let Him Off On a Fifty Dollar Fine and Costs." *Lamar Democrat,* April 12, 1940.

"What We Can Do to Help Lamar." *Lamar Democrat,* August 29, 1929.

"What's the Matter?" *Lamar Democrat,* July 13, 1922.

"What's the Matter with the Courts?" *Lamar Democrat,* March 22, 1923.

"What's the Matter with the Farm?" *Lamar Democrat,* March 11, 1920.

"Who is the Ingrate?" *Lamar Industrial Leader,* September 27, 1901.

"Who Will Get This Piano?" *Lamar Democrat,* October 21, 1909.

"Who's Hurt?" *Lamar Democrat,* April 18, 1901.

"Will George Save Us From Soup?" *Lamar Democrat,* November 13, 1919.

"Wolf in Sheep's Clothing." *Lamar Democrat,* August 1, 1901.

"A Word from Miss Isenhower." *Lamar Democrat,* October 5, 1911.

"A Word from Mrs. Copeland." *Lamar Democrat,* October 5, 1911.

"World Famous Editor Dies." *San Francisco Examiner,* May 9, 1948.

"Would Oust Lake Cemetery Association." *Lamar Democrat,* August 19, 1920.

"Wow! Wow!! Wow!!!" *Lamar Democrat,* December 6, 1923.

"The Yellow Press." *Lamar Democrat,* August 14, 1902.

"Yours Truly in a Crash—When It Rains It Just Naturally Pours." *Lamar Democrat,* November 30, 1934.

"Yours Truly Should Be in New York When You Read This." *Lamar Democrat,* February 11, 1941.

BOOKS

Allen, Charles Laurel. *Country Journalism.* New York: Ronald Press Company, 1928.

Bing, Phil C. *The Country Weekly.* New York: D. Appleton and Company, 1917.

Carroll, Carroll. *None of Your Business: Or My Life with J. Walter Thompson.* New York: Cowles Book Company, 1970.

Clark, Thomas D. *The Southern Country Editor.* Columbia: University of South Carolina, 1991.

Cloud, Barbara. *The Business of Newspapers on the Western Frontier.* Reno: University of Nevada Press, 1992.

Driscoll, Charles B. *The Life of O. O. McIntyre.* New York: Greystone Press, 1938.

Emery, Michael, and Edwin Emery. *The Press and America.* Englewood Cliffs, N.J.: Prentice Hall, 1988.

Faulkner, Harold U. *From Versailes to the New Deal.* New Haven: Yale University Press, 1950.

Faulkner, Virginia, ed. *Roundup: A Nebraska Reader.* Lincoln: University of Nebraska Press, 1957.

Griffith, Sally Foreman. *Home Town News: William Allen White and the Emporia Gazette.* Baltimore: Johns Hopkins University Press, 1989.

Kirkendall, Richard S. *A History of Missouri, Volume V, 1919 to 1953.* Columbia: University of Missouri Press, 1986.

McGovern, James R. *Anatomy of a Lynching: The Killing of Claude Neal.* Baton Rouge: Louisiana State University, 1982.

Morgan, Richard. *J. Walter Takeover: From Divine Right to Common Stock.* Homewood, Ill.: Business One Irwin, 1991.

Mott, Frank Luther. *American Journalism.* New York: Macmillan Company, 1950.

N. W. Ayer and Son's American Newspaper Annual and Directory. Philadelphia: N. W. Ayer and Son, 1900, 1901, 1909, 1911, 1912, 1925, 1941.

Official Manual of the State of Missouri for the Years 1915–1916. Jefferson City, Mo.: Hugh Stephens Printing Company, 1915.

Official Manual of the State of Missouri for the Years 1935–1936. Jefferson City, Mo.: Midland Printing Company, 1935.

Pickett, Calder. *Ed Howe: Country Town Philosopher.* Lawrence: University of Kansas Press, 1968.

Safley, James Clifford. *The Country Newspaper and Its Operation.* New York: D. Appleton and Company, 1930.

Shay, Frank. *Judge Lynch: His First Hundred Years.* Montclair, N.J.: Patterson Smith, 1969.

Siebert, Fredrick Seaton. *The Rights and Privileges of the Press.* Westport, Conn.: Greenwood Press, 1934.

Swindler, William F. *Problems of Law in Journalism.* Westport, Conn.: Greenwood Press, 1955.

Truman, Margaret. *Harry S. Truman.* New York: William Morrow and Company, Inc., 1973.

VanGilder, Marvin L. *The Story of Barton County.* 1972.

White, William Allen. *The Autobiography of William Allen White.* New York: Macmillan Company, 1946.

Young, Reba. *Down Memory Lane.* 1992.

INTERVIEWS, LETTERS, MANUSCRIPTS, SPEECHES

Aull, Arthur. "Advertising." Speech presented at the Twelfth Winter Meeting of the Missouri Press Association at Laclede Hotel in St. Louis, February 9, 1906.

Jones, Richard to Chad Stebbins, November 29, 1994.

Popplewell, Frank S. "Arthur Aull and The Lamar Democrat: A Study in Rural Missouri Journalism in the 1920's." Special Collections, Barton County Historical Society, Lamar, Mo., 1973.

Stebbins, Chad. "A Biography of James C. Kirkpatrick." Master's thesis, Central Missouri State University, 1984.

White, Betty Aull, daughter of Arthur Aull, interview by author, July 6, 1992, Lamar, Mo., tape recording.

White, Betty Aull, daughter of Arthur Aull, interview by author, March 16, 1994, Lamar, Mo., tape recording.

INDEX

tions, 94–95; debut of semi-weekly,
100; advertising editions, 100–101;
preserved on microfilm, 161
Lamar Democrat Publishing Company,
53–54
Lamar Industrial Union, 12
Lamar Journal, 136
Lamar Leader, 10, 11, 12, 13, 14–18, 20,
23, 24, 33, 51, 87, 92, 162
Lamar Republican, 10, 11, 12, 13, 14,
17, 22, 33, 134, 162, 163
Lamar Republican-Sentinel, 51, 74, 77,
87, 92, 162–63
Lamar Sentinel, 10
LeMire, C. P., 81
Libel, criminal, 11, 12, 13, 19, 24, 53
Liberal, Missouri, 4, 70, 97, 98, 118,
129
Liberal Enterprise, 24–25
Liberal News, 108, 134
Life, 2, 37, 46, 57
Literary Digest, 140
Long, Smith, 25
Los Angeles Examiner, 54
Los Angeles Record, 54
Los Angeles Times, 137
Lynch, J. W., 77
Lynch, Jay W., 63, 67–84
Lynch, Leola, 69, 74, 75, 76, 77
Lynch, Maude, 69, 76, 77, 83–84
Lynch, Stella, 76, 77
Lynchings, number of, 78

McAllister, Frank, 81
McCreary, John, 11–12, 14, 19, 24
McCune-Brooks Hospital (Carthage),
128
McDaniel, H. D. (Tige), 128
McGovern, James, 82–83
McIntyre, O. O., 2
McKinley, William, 32
Marriage licenses, 50
Martin, Arthur Aull (great-grandson),
127
Martin, Luanna Noyes (granddaughter),
127, 163
Martin, Thomas W., 4, 6, 7, 21, 22, 23
Mayes, Walter, 4

Mayo Clinic, 132, 133
Medill School of Journalism, 29, 43
Memphis Commercial Appeal, 137
Metropolitan Museum of Art (New
York), 105
Miami Herald, 137
Miller, Sol, 131
Mindenmines, Missouri, 5, 6, 7, 9, 129,
143
Missouri General Assembly, 83
Missouri House of Representatives, 21
Missouri Newspaper Hall of Fame, 137
Missouri-Pacific Railroad, 9, 69, 72
Missouri Press Association, 24, 35, 98,
121, 137
Missouri Press News, 54
Missouri Relief and Construction Com-
mission, 118
Missouri State Penitentiary, 71, 79
Mr. Wu the dog, 129–30, 143
Moberly Democrat (Mo.), 54
Montgomery, J. R., 94
Moore, Edwin L., 14, 19, 20, 21, 22, 23,
25, 53, 131
Moore, Thomas, 122
Mount Vernon, Missouri, 127
Muddy Creek, 9, 31, 105, 123, 126
Mulberry, Kansas, 96
Mulberry Independent, 96

Nashville, Missouri, 3, 4, 5, 143
National Broadcasting Company, 103
Nevada, Missouri, 42, 72, 76, 81, 97
New journalism, 27, 28
New York Journal, 27, 30
New York Times, 1, 78, 119, 162
New York World Telegram, 2
New Yorker, 2
Newsweek, 1, 56
Noble, Bill, 44
Nohrenburg, Otto, 96
North Star School, 4
Northwestern University, 29, 43
Nowlin, J. M., 89
Noyes, Garrett (son-in-law), 127, 128
Noyes, Genevieve (daughter), 64, 121,
126, 127, 128, 143
Noyes, Nancy (granddaughter), 127